The End of Revolution

The End of Revolution:

A New Assessment of Today's Rebellions

by STANLEY P. WAGNER

South Brunswick and New York: A. S. Barnes and Co.
London: Thomas Yoseloff Ltd

A.S. Barnes and Company, Inc.
Cranbury, New Jersey 08512

Thomas Yoseloff Ltd
108 New Bond Street
London W1Y OQX, England

To my wife, Diana,
my daughter, Kathleen,
and in memory of my
mother, Anna

First Printing June, 1970
Second Printing April, 1971

ISBN: 0-498-07381-5
Printed in the United States of America

CONTENTS

Foreword

RATIONALE OF THE BOOK

The book is about urbanism. It maintains that urbanism is an organic form of life, a mature stage of civilization. The United States and Western Europe have achieved this stage of maturity or are near achieving it. The growing stage, the physically, rapidly changing stage of urbanism is coming to an end. The cities, which are the physical forms of urbanism, have been located and their forms of mass and flow reasonably fixed. There will be new cities, but these will largely be to integrate the system and operation of the existing cities. The entrance and egress of cities will follow patterns long established. Passenger air travel will increasingly replace ground transportation, especially on the longer route. But the expansion of the air industry has its physical limits as did that of rail transportation in our past history. In the 1870's the transportation observer might have seen unlimited rail expansion. Yet by the 1890's the railroads were completed in their physical layout and rail mileage. This is happening to our air travel which at the moment may seem limitless. The rest of this century will see Americans on the move but through well-established channels. The propeller-driven planes were the workhorses of the last fifty years. They are being replaced by the jets, which will be the workhorses for a long time to come. The chain of superhighways is also near completion.

The mature urbanism developing in the West carries in its technical capacity the early end to human material wants. The abolition of poverty now already planned for in these countries is feasible in the next decade. The ending of this poverty will present the West with the opportunity of continuing the investment in improved and more luxurious dwellings, increased quantity of food; it will mean improved and faster travel. But it will also offer the option of leisure, recreation, education, and the sharpening of artistic tastes. Instead of faster travel the choice may be for travel at a leisurely walking pace. We may wish to move at a pace at which we can readily see and smell a natural earth in the spring. With a guaranteed existence physically, the choice may be to spend less time at innovation and more time at recreation. There is no productivity on the golf course. There is fellowship, experience, and competitive exhilaration. The chances are great that the speed of travel may purposely be reduced since speed will not be necessary. People will walk farther, bicycle, and if necessary move by jet at six hundred miles an hour. We can do this with decreasing investment.

This awareness of increased opportunity outside of work is being sharply brought to our attention by the American hippie movement. It is not the dope, the filth, and the long hair that really causes us concern. It is the fact that hippies can stay alive in this country, and with a reasonable amount of comfort and satisfaction, at a very small investment in work time. It is also the violation of our Puritan work ethic that frightens us. What further, we ask in a state of high apprehension, can we expect of the next generation, freer from work than this one?

The assumption today of most published authorities blindly subscribes to the fact that we will continue to make the first choice—the continued work investment in the improvement of everything. The evidence is becoming clear to suggest that we are already making a choice against the work ethic. There is an end to increasing investment of material for industrial innovation just as surely as the most advanced industrial societies have shown a reduction in growth in capital goods for consumer goods. Increasing investment for innovation that will occur will be hypothetical model building and simulating projects. This will inexpensively channel the energies of the most creative in the next generation without the necessity of ever increasing production.

The rationale for hard labor and delayed gratification is increasingly more difficult to defend, in America and Western Europe. Mature urbanism in these countries offers an immediate gift of an abundant life for the individual. It is a life relatively free from physical pain and economic worry. It offers beauty, art, and justice before youth has to make any sacrifice of work. It offers an opportunity for self-expression, travel, education and leisure.

Americans and Western Europeans in their homes are only in a vague way beginning to realize this gift of inheritance. They are still motivated by production and pursuit rather than consumption. They still look at change as more hopeful than the *status quo*. Change, even for the sake of change, is still considered progress while stability is feared, especially by the older, depression-reared generation, as a sign of decline and deterioration.

There is relatively no awareness that since the mass introduction of television two decades ago the life of the average American has been affected physically by very slight and superficial change. Each product he buys may have a new label, new design, new color, but the actual product is only slightly modified. Our most basic commodity, the automobile, is fundamentally the same one we purchased after World War II; only the style has changed.

Our imaginations since Sputnik have been captivated by the satellite and outer space travel and possible settlement. But in reality these have no more affected urban life in America and Europe than Admiral Byrd's expeditions to the South Pole in the late twenties. The barren vastness of Antarctica still remains stimulating to imagination but absent from any real colonization and development forty years later. Thus are the space experiments to remain, portent of things to come, but hardly more in this century.

The youths of these countries are more aware of the new conditions than are their parents. They realize that their parents lived in a world where physical work, progress, and limited rewards in a distant future were the basic motivations. These beliefs were realistic when production still required nearly total commitment to work for a modest return of goods and leisure. This older generation, those born before 1940, find it hard to accept a world of urbanism where physical work, progress, and change are no longer basic. They cannot adjust themselves to a life of increased leisure. This is really the only explanation for the most puzzling political phenomenon of the western world. In the past it was always the young who were for more change and more progress. The older one was the less willing he was to change. Today, however, to much of our confusion, the process is reversed.

The political conservatism is more likely to be among the young. They already feel the real choice even though they still cannot verbalize it. They already sense that they can live the abundant life here and now with only a modest commitment to work. Comfort, leisure, and self-fulfillment are no longer a dream to be postponed to the future. Mature urbanism provides it today with a minimum output of work time providing they are willing to accept the physical system essentially as it is, with maintenance only.

This "maintenance only" theme will increasingly be demanded, and there will be a conscious restriction made on revolutionary change. Change will inevitably occur, and in some distant future, in a revolutionary way once again. But for the rest of this century, and possibly the next, change will have to compete with the economy of a comfortable equilibrium—and it will run a poor second.

INTRODUCTION

Jeremy Bentham, one of England's major philosophers, founded his utilitarian school on the principle that nature had placed mankind under the governance of two sovereign masters, pain and pleasure. Despising pain and seeking pleasure, man could, according to Bentham, organize his life intelligently. By adding the total pleasures against the pains in any given action, he could choose the correct action. This formula, he advocated, could be applied to society if only it had sense enough to choose administrators who were honest and who could count. Despite the many difficulties in his simple formula, it broke paths of objective human analysis that helped re-order a great deal of man's life. Bentham failed, however, to realize that there are two even more basic sovereigns on which the yardstick of pain and pleasure are ordered. These are self-consciousness and memory, which more truly denote man qua man than does pleasure or pain. Without self-consciousness and memory, there is neither physical nor mental pain. With them, man experiences pleasure and pain, not only of the present and future, but also of the past, not only physical but intellectual. But far more significant is that self-consciousness and memory permit man to understand the objective world, the world of non-self and non-present. They permit him not only to rationally organize his own life, but also the structure of the universe itself.

15

The first non-self thing that self-consciousness and memory-making man comes to understand is that the world is in a state of flux, of eternal change. He saw the seasons change and found that his food supply depended upon many uncertain forces in the world. Nor could man have been conscious long before he was aware of change in himself and his off-spring; past pleasures became pains, and pains pleasures. A rich source of food supply or water might be curtailed by nature or by other humans. This law of change is a vital part of human existence, and from every indication will continue to determine our lives for a long time to come.

Consciousness and memory have not been limited to recording change. They have also made man aware of the opposite, that there are certain constants in life, things repeat themselves, and that keeping track of such repetition permits one to anticipate and to prepare life more intelligently. This conscious quest for order is perhaps the single activity that most distinguishes man from other species. As soon as man becomes conscious of some order in nature, he is ready and desirous of more. This has caused man to jump to premature conclusions, to refuse to recognize evidence contrary to his hoped-for order, to be a creature of habit and prejudice, and voluntarily to suffer great pain in the expectation of arriving at the eternal order. He thus refuses to know himself in terms of pain and pleasure alone, and to act upon Bentham's dictum. He is conscious of a world outside himself which also constitutes the basis of behavior: at the same time that the individual seeks pleasure, he is also seeking a world order.

Hence, as soon as the individual or group can manage, they try to establish order and stability in their lives. The male is assigned to hunting, the women to making raiment and preparing meals. Some are assumed to be hewers of wood, while others are sowers of grain. Some are assigned to be carpenters and others warriors, churchmen or rulers. And woe to those who might try to violate the order. Even the critics are in danger if they should call attention to phenomena that is counter to the purported order, and to go further and offer alternatives. The history of mankind has been the search for the imposition of order on life whenever that order made any sense at all. The order was kept as long as physically possible, until the contradictions, the disturbances, the pain became so unbearable, and imposed order so illogical that all or some of the old order was changed, and disorder temporarily embraced. Therefore the desire to predict, to live with certainty, is there in man's consciousness as a basic determinant in ordering his life as soon as a formula has any indication of being reasonably accurate and practical.

While the history of an individual may be the search for pleasure and the avoidance of pain, the history of man as a conscious animal is the record of the discovery of order and the ordering of his life accordingly. This history has naturally provided long stretches of ordered life. Discoveries, innovations, and calamities have been unsettling, but usually could be explained or treated as an aberration and not a true violation of a practiced order. This has been true for most of man's history, because great changes, innovations, in his way of living have seldom burst the bonds of traditional order so violently or extensively that an entirely new order had to be created. The more common have been practically imperceptible changes of order. The history of man has experienced only three great revolutions. These are the revolutions of hu-

man life which took place from the savage-collector to the
nomadic-folk societies, to the agri-provincial and finally
to the recent urban-universal. These gigantic revolutions
left little residue of order from the old to the new and
took several generations in occurring. The more prev-
alent "palace revolution" or technical innovation type
of change provided relatively few alterations as compared
to the gigantic revolution of human life which demanded
a radical re-ordering of life. Those who lived through
these periods tried to find order to such a degree that
they even experimented with trying to make chaos and
innovation an order itself. They tried to accustom themselves to accepting the unpredictable, and new, as common. They taught this to their children, and created
philosophies which proclaimed a human contradiction,
the refusal to accept order as the most truly human act.
And they tried to limit the word freedom only in terms
of the new. This was a palliative which could assuage
the anxiety of human beings only as long as they felt
ignorant and helpless as sailors without a compass or rud-
der on the high seas. However, once the basic revolution
had run its course and established man on a new scale of
life, human ordering was again possible, and someone
could improvise a route. The stampede for an end to
revolution was on again.

This book is an attempt to put these two basic challenges of change and order in perspective. They have been
gravely distorted by the revolutionary period through
which we have passed. Our perspective today in the thinking that change and disorder will constantly accelerate as
they have in the recent past is as mistaken as was the pre-
modern period when it assumed the finality of the agricultural order. This book is an attempt to extricate us

from the myth that man could or must become a permanently revolutionary being. The thesis that follows is a
statement of something we are beginning to know em-
pirically but not yet intellectually, that is, the leveling-off
of the urban-universal revolution, especially in the United
States and Western Europe. Once this is more apparent,
the human choice will be for life, comfort, and order over
uncertainty and change, even if the latter might con-
ceivably add an ion of knowledge to the structure of the
world. The new "high priests" for order will assume their
authority and the new "philosophers" will once again
establish an absolute order. This self-consciousness, with
human prejudice for certainty, life and comfort, will speed
the end of revolution.

Part I
The End of Revolution

1. THE MYTH OF PERMANENT REVOLUTION

i. *The Present Perspective of Rapid Change*

The predominant impression that the student of the present receives is that it is a time of swift change, of new modes and products which tend to become obsolete even before they are taken off the drawing boards and put into production. Thus, attempts to predict the things to come are in terms of an ever-accelerating cycle. If it took the population forty years to double, then the predicted exponential is that it will take only twenty in the next time span. If the automobile, radio and television altered our whole way of life in the past half century it supposedly will only take two decades for entirely new inventions to do the same. We hear that in a decade from now half of our present jobs will be obsolete and that our store of knowledge will have doubled. One accepts the sad feeling that the latest model is only a fleeting moment from obsolescence, and the human body but a vestigial remain before complete transformation to a new organism. Small wonder that we are placing such a low value on anything today, including life itself.

The overemphasis on revolution prevents us from having an intelligent estimate of gradual growth, stability and decadence. We overlook the things that remain stable or change very imperceptibly. Gross national product measurements of the American economy, for example, have indicated a slowing down of the rate of growth for some time in recent years. The absolute growth rate of mature economies ranges around three to four percent per year, but it had been triple that in earlier stages. Yet we go on to believe that this reduced expansion is only a very temporary aberration due to some external or internal evil, and that a healthy economy should be expanding at an increasing rate.[1]

This decelerating condition manifests itself in other mature industrial economies of Western Europe as well. While there are some significant and temporary exceptions like that of France, Italy, and especially Western Germany after the Second World War when their growth rate reached percentages known only in premature industrial systems, it must be remembered that the devastation of these countries put them physically in a more primitive stage of growth. But since mentally and psychologically they were mature economies, the move back was rapid, and with maturity they again are faced with a decreased growth rate.

The same kind of decreasing rate of growth and accompanying ignorance of the condition is also evident in these highly industrialized countries which are now experiencing a decline in the rate of population growth. While some of this decline has been obscured by internal migration from rural areas to urban areas, by external migration from less developed to more developed areas, and also by the exploding population base in underdeveloped countries in transition, there is, nevertheless, a clear indication of decreased population growth rates in highly urbanized countries and especially in highly urbanized areas. Yet the thought that a nation's population might be fixed at a given number is still a relatively foreign idea in an advanced country like the United States. Fortunately, the fear of a stable population is not entertained by all of the developing nations. Japan and India have made it a national goal. While a few in America admire them, the thought to most Americans that we might permanently remain with a stabilized population of 250 million appears catastrophic. Somehow, population growth, like all other change, is still equated with the need for growth, which is *ipso facto* associated with some hoped for good. The fact that population growth is increasingly a threat is only beginning to dawn on us.

Perhaps the strongest evidence illustrating a condition of continuous and escalating innovation has been in the realm of automation. Books and articles abound on the subject, breaking it down to a vocabulary all its own, from cybernetics to older terms with new meanings like "feedback" and "data processing." Automation has been heralded as the successor to the industrial revolution, and the predictions are that its development and effects will change our lives even more extensively than the steam engine or electricity. Essentially the automative process promises to have machines replace man in his work, first in his physical work and then, through computer brains, in his mental work. With automated knowledge and automated production there will be no slowdowns due to human idiosyncrasies like coffee breaks or strikes. And where the human is very limited in the factual knowledge he can acquire, retain or handle, the machine is not. The only unanswerable question appears to be, what will be left for humans to do, and especially why such an unlimited number of them?

There is an implied assumption by those who feel auto-

mation will proceed unrestrained that man wants variation and change above everything else; that he will surrender peace of mind, sustenance of body, art, music,
love, and order to his insatiable lust for change and
variation. I carefully use the words "change and variation" rather than the word "knowledge" which we tend
to use more irresponsibly. It is possible that man would
give up a good deal of the earthly pleasures for "true"
knowledge. But the greatest activity of additional automation is far more of a concern with innovation than it is
with knowledge. Therefore somewhere along the line of
our productivity someone is going to say, "I don't want
anything new today, I am perfectly content with what
I have." And when this happens, quality and heritage will
usurp the place of quantity and innovation.

For such a negative attitude toward change and innovation ever to occur again in America seems extremely re-
mote, at least under normal conditions. We can visualize
it under a tyrannical dictatorship like that of the Soviet
Union, or by physical holocaust like that of an atomic
war, but not in a Western industrial nation without either
of the two above. Thus, a condition of leveling off, of
stability, is given little consideration. The myth and the
bias on behalf of change so completely covers our thoughts,
that we refuse to recognize any but this prevailing notion.
We refuse to recognize the possibility that the present
conditions might someday be found satisfactory.

The absurdity that innovation and acceleration pro-
pelled by science and technology will carry us to a promised land has been neatly and humorously illustrated by
one of the leading historians of science, Derek Price.[2] He
shows that at the present rate of reckoning, acceleration
of the production of scientists indicates that in a couple

of centuries there will theoretically be dozens of scientists for every man, woman, child and dog on this planet. In plotting the present exponential production of electrical engineers in America, Price estimates that the entire working population would have to be employed in this field.[3] Using the more serious side of Price's calculations in an area that might be most akin to the measurement of the growth of knowledge is his graph on the historical growth of Western universities. He shows that the growth in numbers of universities was exponential from the year 1200 until 1450, and then stabilized until the nineteenth century when a new exponential growth begin.[4] It will level off in the twentieth century.

ii. *Soviets and Americans Seek the Image of Revolution*

The acceptance of our times as being characterized by revolutionary changes has an unusual vogue of agreement, not only within the highly urbanized countries, but also in the so-called under-developed countries. The persuasiveness of the view of revolutionary change is even more startling when one realizes that two of the most antagonistic and competitive political and economic systems in the world are fully agreed upon the value of it. Conservatives and liberals in the communist and democratic capitalist countries not only accept revolutionary change as characteristic of our times and of the future, but vigorously compete for the image of being the country most capable of revolutionary change.

The Soviets, following Marx's dictum of leading a "permanent revolution," have tried to aggrandize for communism alone the face of continuous change.[5] Their argument is that capitalism reaches a stage of rigidity and inflexibility so that the owners of capital which has been made obsolete by new discoveries resist these discoveries when their investment is threatened. Hence, owners of private railroads resist transportation innovations that might make their private property obsolete. The followers of Marx further project this into a "capitalist" monopolization of property which makes resistance more powerful to economic innovation. While their theory of "economic determinism" operates against any non-economically based human direction, they nevertheless believe that human organization can resist economic determinism for a while under capitalist organization. This is the reason for the communists' confidence that all they need to do is wait until the capitalist system becomes monopolized, rigid, and resistant to change; it then will fall of its own weight to the laws of history, economic determinism and the communist society's willingness to make rapid change.

The Soviets, following Marx's doctrine of permanent revolution, believe that their system of social organization will offer no resistance to technological innovation. They preach that by communizing all property they destroy a natural tendency of humans to try to conserve what is permanently and privately theirs. Thus, they believe that an individual without private property, but simply relying upon the fruits of the productive mechanism alone, cannot, in a sense, fall in love with the productive mechanism because it is not his. In this kind of system the Soviets believe that the individual and the system become not only willing but eager to change the productive mechanism when something better comes along. They do not take stock of any social-psychological consequences since in their minds the material means of production is the fundamental basis of social life and organization. Nor do they trouble themselves as to how an idea like capitalism can for so long frustrate economic determinism.

American liberals and conservatives, on the other hand, are not shy about revolutionary change and claim the title of the most revolutionary nation for themselves. In fact, a book first published by a conservative magazine recently claimed the same title of "Permanent Revolution."[6] There is no ground, therefore, according to most liberal and conservative American interpreters of its tradition, to assume that the United States has, or is becoming, resistant to change. It was a nation born in revolution, and has had a history of revolutionary changes. From one of its main political disciples, Thomas Jefferson, it has maintained that each new generation has the right to completely revise its way of life and destiny. And furthermore, Jeffersonians continue to hold that the living generation has no right to order its own life in such a way as to place a heavy determining burden upon its children.[7]

The freedom from tradition, we in America generally believe, has been fully respected by a full offer of constitutional change to the new voter, by low government indebtedness, and by rapid change in government through frequent elections. Economically, acceptance of change has been guaranteed by maintaining competition, anti-monopoly laws and redistributing wealth by income and inheritance taxes.

The attack is carried to the Soviets by the same interpreters of the American revolutionary tradition by claiming that the Soviets are actually the reactionary and counterrevolutionary ones. By destroying private property the Soviets supposedly return to a system of political despotism which professes interest in change but accomplishes the opposite by stifling the initiative which is purportedly necessary to create and produce something because man personally will benefit from it. Furthermore, it is argued that central allocation of responsibility, even though designed to accept innovation and change, breaks down of its own complexity. Thus, we maintain that the Soviets unwittingly restrain the emergence of the new by curtailing incentive and over-centralizing.

Which is correct, or are both wrong? The proof is in the pudding, and so both nations are now locked in a struggle to illustrate to themselves and to the world that each can change faster than the other. Thus, each innovation in the newest field of endeavor, the space race, is announced as an example of the nation's adaptation to change.

The point here is that there is no shyness, no question about the importance of change, only a strong desire to adapt quickly to new discoveries. The major dispute here appears to be in regard to which political and economic system will most readily accept and promote change. The fact that both may be nearing a plateau of stability is not relished or planned upon as the next stage of social-economic development. Only change and more change is considered a "good thing," claims one of these nations' most astute observers of the current scene.[8]

iii. *Revolution Defined*

The question still needs to be asked as to whether there is a common understanding regarding the terms "revolutionary change" or whether the term has as varied connotations as the term "democracy." It has been readily applied to the contest between the American colonies and England, to the series of upheavals in Paris that became known as the French Revolution, and to the series of rebellions against authority in Russia that gives title to their revolution. All of these implied violence, all essentially were a challenge and overthrow to the existing authority, and all of these changed drastically the fundamental nature of the authority itself.

The term "revolutionary change" is, however, not limited to contests with human authority. It is readily used to describe a form of change or alteration in other areas. Perhaps the most common connotation has been its association with the development of industry in the late eighteenth century. It has also been applied to the expansion of world commerce during the latter part of the fifteenth century. More recently we see it used in the urbanization of the world or in the substituting of Einstein's theory of relativity for Newtonian physics. Therefore, we are forced to answer whether there is something common about all of these revolutions, and also whether the use of this term can be accepted along some uniform lines. In order to provide the answer we need to give some attention to the anatomy of the term.

iv. *Two Stages of Revolution*

There must be two stages of change in order for a revolution to have taken place. We assume first, a condition of things in effect, and working. This can be the authority of aristocratic and imperial England over her colonies. It can be the exercise of hereditary monarchy of the tsar over the people of Russia. It can be the organization of livelihood on an agricultural, or commercial basis or both. Or it can be intellectual authority like the reliance for answers about life upon reason and authority. So, to begin with there must be an operating or functioning system, a condition of equilibrium.

Following the condition of equilibrium, for a revolution to begin there must be an appearance of a totally different method of order which gives evidence of performing certain fundamental life processes, or survival and well-being more efficiently than the method in use. This brings into effect man's critical sense which demands the more efficient method, his self conscious desire for order.

There is then the second stage of change which is the violent stage. It is not, as we wrongly suppose, always an extremely rapid change. There is the connotation sometimes derived when it is contrasted with the evolutionary process. A revolution is always evolutionary in that it has a genesis of growth, and it is usually evolutionary in that it may take a hundred years or more before it is completed. Nor does the violence imply the shooting of people. Its violent nature is in the death, the final extinction of the previous condition, method or authority which had been fundamental in life. The end of the revolution —which, in its etymological sense means to rotate or come back a full circle—will provide a new supplier of the necessities which had previously been supplied by the process, authority or method now in extinction. It also implies that when the change is fully complete there is an "end to that revolution." There is no reason or evidence to suppose that at the moment the new process has won ascendency it will immediately be challenged or replaced.[9]

In examining the previously cited revolutions we can notice the two stages of the American Revolution. It substituted an authority based on "consent and performance" for one based on heredity. The extinction of the monarchical authority required extensive fighting in this case, but it would still have been a revolution if the end had been accomplished without fighting. This was the case with Britain's own "Glorious Revolution," which substituted the authority of Parliament for that of the monarch. It is rather notable that both of these revolutions attained conditions of long political stability.

The French Revolution also substituted consent and performance for heredity as the basis of holding high political office. The same was essentially true of the initial Russian Revolution, although the Russian people were immediately cast into a further revolution by conscious design of the new leaders. This extended revolution demanded the transfer of population from rural to urban areas and from very primitive traditional mentality based on mysticism and magic to one that was based entirely upon science. Throwing all these drastic changes at the Russian people at once was an extremely painful process. The apparent logic for this extension of chaos was as follows: (1) Its leaders wanted to reduce the time span of overall revolution by ninety percent. This provided a logic for all variations from the tried and true systems of Britain and America toward industrial development. (2) Born in war, starvation, revolution, and extremely primitive conditions of livelihood, all change toward the new or even back to the old order would still have been painful. Thus, the inclusion of pain to bring the new was not as vehemently opposed as it might have been if the old order could have been restored without too much pain. Why the Russian people permitted or bore the heavier pain for a short period as opposed to a lighter pain over a longer period will undoubtedly remain highly controversial. The reader should not assume that there is any implication of success for the short heavy pain route. The only success implied is the adoption of this method. Undoubtedly, the Russian leaders were very capable at selling their messianic propaganda far out of proportion to the benefits received. Bentham's organization of life on the pleasure-pain principle was certainly disregarded for a long time in Soviet Russia.

The primitive state of the Russian system before the revolution is often ignored in examining the logic of the Soviet revolution. The Russians had practically no urban base to which they could return psychologically as did the Germans after World War II. Furthermore, the Russian civilization had never gone through a religious revolution comparable to the Protestant Revolution, nor a political one comparable to the Glorious Revolution in Britain, or to the American Revolution. Thus, they did not have their agricultural civilization based on reason, logic, or common sense which is more compatible with science.[10] By trying to cut the time of the revolutionary process very sharply, the Soviet leaders have dramatized extreme suffering to the Western world and have made the process of revolution itself suspect, at least to the developed Western nations, regardless of how desirable and inevitable its directions might be.[11]

v. *How Permanent Is the Permanent Revolution?*

With this explication of what appears to be the prevailing thought, the main theme should be resumed; the idea that the permanent revolution, supposedly begun in 1776 or 1917, is to increase in momentum. Therefore, it is agreed, those societies which adjust to constant and accelerating revolutionary change are to inherit the leadership of the world. The new order, if such is possible, in this thinking is to institutionalize change. This, of course, is a total contradiction to stability and should not be permitted to confuse the reader. Should the stage be reached where change accelerates so fast that everything thought of is obsolete before it can be put into production, this

can hardly be thought of as an ordered, stable, and pre-
dictable process without destroying the distinction between a stage of revolution and nonrevolution. If either
one of the two explanations of "permanent revolution" is
accepted, then human life from now on must be increasingly chaotic since the intensity of the fundamental
changes can only continue to increase. At some point
there must come a time when the only choice will be between the obsolete methods or authorities. What then
will be the criteria for choice? Man would have to live in
a totally unpredictable world, without standards, subject
to chance inventions, slave to the new, simply because it
is new. It could end in degeneration of humanity, barbarism, and eventual destruction. It is inconceivable that
man would not try to reverse such a direction.

It is small wonder then, that people are actually beginning to recoil from the thought of the future. It also
serves as an explanation of why self-destruction plays such
a large role in our thoughts today. Man, who would have
to live with the total uncertainty of the morrow could
hardly bear to take a step today. And if self-destruction
is not to be the consequence, only a radical altering of
the biology of man, perhaps in the nature of Huxley's
Brave New World, is the logical alternative. But if it is
to be assumed that man and the physical environment has
certain boundaries, then it must be concluded that a condition of equilibrium, substantial stability, and relatively
no change has been, and should continue to be fundamental to the individual and to the group.

Let us, therefore, return to the less obvious part of the
idea of revolution and not treat it as permanent, but
rather as being limited to a certain span of time. Presume
that the many changes—revolutions, if you will—are only

segments of a much larger revolution which will be completed. This revolution must be big enough to encompass the many smaller ones already discussed. Such a revolution by its nature must be not only a physical one but also a mental one. The revolution referred to by the author of this book is the collectivization and/or urbanization of the people, on the one hand, which is the physical revolution, plus the universalization of the people's thought processes and values on the other. It is one that began about the beginning of the nineteenth century and is being completed in countries like the United States, England, Holland, and others, in the latter part of the twentieth century. It had its precursors in the earlier scientists like Copernicus and Newton or the primitive collectivities known as cities long before then, but its full implementation is of very recent vintage.

The date of 1800 is only a convenient separation. One could begin with the first census taken in the United States in 1790, Robert Malthus' essay on population in 1798, or as Nathan Glazer indicates, the British census of 1801 which, according to Glazer, reflected a widespread desire to know accurately the facts of population increase and decrease. The rise of the science of statistics about the turn of the nineteenth century and its application to society was the birth of the revolution of social science which, until then, affected society only indirectly.[12]

The urbanization of the world began at approximately the same period of time as the development of rapid inland transportation. Prior to that time cities were always limited to areas with accessible waterways. It is difficult to visualize urbanization without science and it is equally difficult to see the scientific developments of the nineteenth and twentieth centuries without urbanization.

Neither urbanization nor science was developed on any scale before that time. That is, they were not threats to the replacement of life on the farm by the urbanite, nor of the man of letters by the man of the laboratory. In 1800, the die was cast and the whole complexity of the rural-common-sense civilization has since been in the process of being extinguished by the urban-science civilization. This new civilization has its goals, its boundaries, its limitations, and a rationale of order, just as the preceding civilization had. Thus, both the Western capitalist and the communist nations make a grave mistake in assuming the "permanent revolution" and they frustrate themselves by it. It is a dangerous myth. It is like changing from a car to a plane while both are in motion, making the change only because the latter is going faster and not asking where it is going, and whether we want to go there, or whether we might get there sooner and safer by walking. It fails to take cognizance of the new order that is rapidly implanting itself despite the fears of those who were the leaders in fighting the old order. Their fears are generated by the belief that a new order is nothing more than the resurrection of the old obsolete order. They confuse the process, the means, with the ends, which is a great fallacy. There certainly was a need to rid ourselves of the old order, now obsolete, but not of order per se. The rural organization was no longer viable, but an order of urban-science as a basis is desirable and essential.

Notes: Chapter 1

1. W. W. Rostow, *The Stages of Economic Growth* (Cambridge, Mass., Cambridge University Press, 1962) Chapter 6, provides for a fundamental insight into this area. He recognizes the problem of the end of revolutionary growth and raises the

question of what will we in America choose when the mature economy can supply our physical needs. However, Rostow too is more in love with rapid growth than stability and indirectly expresses a concern that the absence of growth might bore us to death.

2. Derek Price, *Science Since Babylon* (New Haven, Conn., Yale University Press, 1961), p. 113.
3. *Ibid.*, p. 108.
4. *Ibid.*, p. 115.
5. Karl Marx first argued the "permanent revolution" theory in "Address To The Communist League" 1850, and it has remained consistently a part of communist ideology with the usual variations that affect communist theory.
6. The editors of *Fortune*, in collaboration with Russell W. Davenport, *The Permanent Revolution* (New York, Prentice-Hall, 1951).
7. *The Wisdom of Thomas Jefferson*, Ed. by Edward Boykin (Garden City, N.Y., Doubleday, 1943).
8. Dennis W. Brogan, *The Price of Revolution* (New York, Harper, 1951), pp. vii and 1.
9. This is one of the naive assumptions of Hegel and Marx in their acceptance of the dialectic method of social analysis.
10. Alfred North Whitehead in his *Science and The Modern World* shows how crucial this thought had been to the development of science in Germany.
11. This, of course, does not mean that the time span from the agri-provincial to the urban-universal Revolution has to be in keeping with the West. It depends upon the level of collectivization and science already in existence. Take Japan, for example, that was able to make the transfer in a very short period of time. While its mental climate was not far removed from that of the Russians, it was far more urbanized and had a far easier basis for urbanizing more rapidly because of the size of the country geographically.
12. David Lerner, editor, *The Human Meaning of the Social Sciences* (New York, Meridian Books, 1959), the article especially by Nathan Glazer, "The Rise of Social Research in Europe."

2. THE CONDITION OF STABILITY IN HISTORY

Measuring whether a revolution is ending or whether it is accelerating is the central question in this chapter. In so far as it is possible, the attempt will be made to consider it within the framework of the methodology of the social sciences. The presentation of the hypothesis and the supporting evidence will be made in such a way as to permit empirical verification of the material. A word of caution needs to be said here that would prevent a built-in bias of the social sciences from operating in the evaluation.

i. Recent Emergence of the Social Sciences and Their Bias against Stability

The reader must remember that the social sciences have emerged only within the past half century.[1] They are part of the most recent revolution in history, the "urban-universal" which has occurred within the United States, England and a few other countries within the past hundred years. Since the greatest enemy of the social scientists in developing their methods and fields of specialization has been tradition, traditional ways and the study of history, their rebellion has been most vehement in this direction. Their studies and experiments have been primarily of the current scene, the revolutionary scene.

Also their studies have been restricted towards subject experiments in the intranational scene. This limitation was a consequence of the political dictates rather than scientific preference. While they undoubtedly have been extremely fruitful in their results, especially for practical immediate nationalistic application, they have, in turn, obstructed the developent of theory in cross national and in long time span periods. The social scientists' resistance to history is not necessarily as a negative bias or the refusal to use it in the verification of their findings, but rather in failing to appreciate the possibility of a different milieu. The "theory of progress" imprisoned them to view change as development. They have lost sight of fundamental law in history—the law of leveling off after revolution, of reaching plateaus of relative stability, of following a given line of direction with only alterations and modifications rather than drastic change and acceleration. Their nationalistic bias obscured similarities in cultures which would emphasize stability and uniformity rather than revolution and versatility.

Certain of the social sciences have been more exposed to change than others, although all are heavily influenced by their new emergence in the revolutionary period in which they find themselves. The impression that the economist, psychologist, or sociologist gets of change and the rate of change is not only of the possibility of it but of the inevitability of it in his own lifetime. Being born and reared in revolution, it is difficult to imagine that things could move more slowly. View the development of psychology struggling on the one hand to extricate itself from the "soul," as interpreted traditionally, to "psyche" that can be experimented with scientifically. During the same period the agricultural-provincial world has gone through the most extensive change in the attitudes and practices regarding sex that historical man has yet faced. It is small wonder that the studies by psychologists with this area lead them to state their hypothesis in terms of change rather than stability.

The sociologists and economists find themselves in much the same position. While both are struggling to liberate themselves from the agricultural-provincial dogma, they are cast into a tremendous revolution brought about by the collectivization of people and universalization and scientification of their mentality. The sociologist who has given heavy preoccupation to the study of the structure and function of the family discovers that almost everything said about the rural family alters in the urbanized family organization. This is also true in areas like race or class or caste. All are in a transitional stage where they are re-emerging in different forms.

The economist can perhaps be blamed least in his preoccupation with the present and its acceleration, with his over emphasis on economic growth and undervaluing of economic stability. First, the economists have never recovered from Marx's economics which put a premium on technological change. Since Marxian technology was relatively independent of human control all attempts at technological stabilization by social-political efforts were considered downright ridiculous. Therefore, all traditionalists are the natural enemies of Marxian economists. They are viewed as Don Quixotes fighting nonexistent enemies. Second, the urban-universal revolution has been most explosive in the area of study by the economist. The productive capacities of sub-national and national groups have mutiplied so rapidly that unlimited productivity has been accepted as an unqualified good. It has taken a myth-breaking book like Kenneth Galbraith's *The Affluent Society* to call this to question. However, Galbraith does not question economic growth. He only questions whether the direction we now pursue is intelligent for growth in the long run.

The political scientist, especially in Britain and America, and the historian have not been caught up as extensively in the present revolution as have the other sciences. There have been relatively minor alterations and modifications in their subject matter, the American and British political structure. The political systems of these two countries have, in fact, been paragons of stability and perhaps stratification in this world of revolution. The historian, with a natural reluctance to study people still living, spends most of his time on the events that preceded the urban-universal revolution and so he is not caught up in the study of change. While both political science and history have broken from the earlier non-scientific schools they are not as affected by the present condition of acceleration.

However, while these two disciplines could contribute more to the place of stability as a factor in the study of social and political organization, they also neglect it. The only apparent explanation for this appears to be the self doubt that arises from such consideration since it is so markedly out of step with the rest of the social sciences. Therefore, a great number of the historians and political scientists subscribe to the theory of progress just as religiously and look at stability suspiciously, as something that is past or that needs to be altered. Arnold Toynbee, in his monumental *A Study of History,* is one of the few brave souls in the recent period who undertook to create a general theory of growth and decay of civilization, but he did not concern himself with the significance of stability in the history of man. In political science, such leaders in America as David Easton, Hannah Arendt, and E. A. Shils, emphasize the lack of non-nationalistic time perspective but provide only a partial explanation of the present period. Their theories of equilibrium rely too heavily upon the intellectual side and too little upon the physical determinants.

ii. *Conditions Associated with Stability*

In order to demonstrate that a new period of order and stability, a new pleateau, may soon be feasible for man, it becomes imperative that we indicate the conditions under which it will take place. To do this, we must first take a close examination of the conditions that are always found in association with those societies in history which are in a state of stability. Second, it is important to demonstrate that the present revolutionary condition is one of recent vintage and not four thousand years old, as most historians and social scientists would have us believe. If it is four thousand years old, it would be naïve to assume that it might end in five or ten years in any part of the world. Third, for a verification of growing stability in the present, it is imperative to demonstrate that those conditions always associated with stability in the past are reappearing in our society. Finally, one must make neither the Marxian nor the Hegelian mistake of permitting either the intellectual or the economic process to overbalance the other. This section will attempt to demonstrate the first point, i.e., that a given set of conditions accompany stability and that any examination of historical periods of stability would support the assumptions of this thesis.

While the preceding chapter took some time to define revolution, a few words here need to be said about the condition of life that is not in revolution, but in a state of equilibrium, of stability. *Webster's New World Dictionary* defines stability as the "capacity of an object to return to equilibrium or to its original position after having been displaced." The intent of this definition and explication is to describe a condition which is alive and vital but retains its basic form. If it is replaced by an entirely different form, then we have a revolution.

The application of the term stability to the individual or society should encompass all conditions of life, physical and mental. There should be little desire for change either because there is contentment with the existing conditions or ignorance of things being done differently. The primary ethos would be protection of the status quo. There would be sufficient satisfaction to accept the given order and prepare its off-spring to live the same way. Stability, it should be remembered, does not mean a reaction to the past. It is an attempt to hold the present.

iii. *Pre-Conditions for Stability*

The first precondition for stability therefore must be a set of physical conditions that remain basically the same and do not force the system to look for new ways of dealing with new conditions. An example of this would be where agriculture continues to be the basic method of making a living even though a war or "palace revolution" might provide a temporary dislocation of life by ruining crops or preventing them from being cultivated. The important point of stability is the relative sameness of the physical world, of production and distribution, of social structure, of a psychological cognizance of stability and desire to return to it. The change which always has to be there to some extent would be only a superficial change, like that of human faces. This kind of change is not fundamental to society even though it is for the individual.

The second pre-condition for stability is a well-developed hierarchical authority. This is essential to a stable society since it is impossible for any social organization to function without some differences about property, and services rendered. John Locke, one of the great political philosophers who began with the assumption of the peaceful and cooperative nature of man, still could not conceive of people living together for any period of time without having differences over property. So, even for Locke there had to be enough authority for at least the purpose of providing judges and a court system to settle disputes. He was then faced with the problem of creating authority which could identify, maintain and remove authority with some degree of stability. Although it should be remembered that Locke was favoring a revolutionary period and was trying to reduce authority to a bare minimum. Had he been concerned with stability, hierarchical authority would necessarily have been to the maximal side of the scale.

The ideal system for stability in authority would be a caste or class system where the role the individual was to play was not determined by some nonarbitrary method like birth, into a class by some physical or intellectual classification like I.Q. over which there is no recourse. The sociologists refer to an extreme of this condition with the non value term "stratification." Arnold Toynbee, whose value orientation was more toward change than stability, labels such a condition as an "arrested" civilization. The connotation, however, even by the sociologists, associated with these was that as long as class and caste resist change they are harmful. There is a tendency to overlook class and caste as also beneficial providing they are able to handle disturbances. This would be especially true if the end pursued was contentment with life rather than innovation, since the latter can seldom be realized without considerable anxiety, frustration and challenge to existing authority.

A third precondition associated with stability is the *high* prominence of traditional or rather voluntary authority, as contrasted with political or compulsory authority. There appears to be no dispute in social science circles on this point, i.e., that traditional authority is a conservative factor, limiting change. It necessarily binds together the past, the present, and the future. This is why Edmund Burke, the great conservative political philosopher, gave it such a prominent place in his philosophy. This is why the conservative movement in American politics or economics can at least always agree on the importance of tradition.

Thus, an attack on traditional authority by Marx was in keeping with his desire to promote change. Since Marx assumed that this was to be a permanent revolution, there was never to be any place for traditional authority. It is true that in the ideal Marxian state whatever authority existed was to be a non-compulsory one. However, in practice, Marxism always turns out to be associated with a high level of political or compulsory authority. This is one of the great weaknesses of Marxism. He missed the real function of traditional authority. It is not just the fact that traditional authority conserves, protects the past and the status quo, but that as an order that appears natural, operating without pressure and compulsion it must of necessity be hierarchical, fixed, and with the trappings of class. Stability has its merits and of course, its price.

iv. *Three Fundamental Revolutions and Stability*

In viewing revolution and change, it is possible to misjudge incidental variations for the basic character of the fundamental revolution, i.e., that which provides the basis of life, physically and mentally. There have been only three such revolutions in the recorded history of man. The first was the emergence of man as a collector, gatherer, hunter, with a very limited basis of communication with others. This was the nomadic-folk revolution. Stability in this type of society was found as long as the members remained essentially nomadic-folk. While they encountered a great variety of problems, such as shortage of game or berries causing starvation or conflict with other groups for food resources, their basic organization did not change. As long as they returned to their nomadic-folk stage their society could be considered stable physically and mentally. They had problems, great problems, but they recognized them and knew whether they could deal with them or not. They could point to the great number of things which were stable and orderly and erase the temporary inconvenience as some punishment of God or evil spirit for some earlier violation of order. Their physical environment was static as far as they personally could make any change. Their social class structure inevitably emerged as an hereditary one even though a new hereditary conqueror might take over. Their search for direction was from the authority of past experience.

The second great revolution came when man as a farmer, a cultivator, a domesticator, a settled peasant arrived on the scene. He kept records and passed on a written tradition. This was the agricultural-provincial revolution. It occurred about 5,000 B.C. and in a relatively short time displaced the nomadic-folk societies in most of the habitable and cultivable places in the world. New order and stability then took place for the greater part of seven thousand years of human history. Humans, personalities, lived and died by the millions, but their containers of order were surprisingly uniform. The agricultural-provincial order imposed itself upon individuals. Now the agricultural order has been disturbed as the nomadic-folk was disturbed. The problems of soil-exhaustion, overpopulation, and technological development have forever disturbed rural life in the world. But until the nineteenth century all of these changes did not replace the fundamental agricultural-provincial life until a new form, the urban-universal was the unquestioned conqueror. The farmer of A.D. 1700 still had more in common with the farmer of 1700 B.C. in his physical life and mental outlook than he did with the urbanized food producer of the twentieth century. Plato and Ben Franklin would have far more in common than Ben Franklin and the American of today. The industrial development, until the latter nineteenth century, was constantly integrated into agricultural life, made subordinate to it until the changes it was bringing about were entirely unincorporable into the agricultural order. Then the bonds burst in the Western world and a new order would have to replace it.

The third great revolution, the urban-universal which began sometime in the nineteenth century, in an irreversible way is now coming to an end in the United States, England, and other urbanized countries in the mid-twentieth century. The order of urban science with an urbanized scientized people making this the basis for mental outlook, are organizing themselves with a certainty that life will remain at this stage. If cities are destroyed by bombing or hurricanes then cities will be replaced. Once the people educate themselves to the urban-universal mentality they can feel confident that there will only be minor adjustments to be made. There will be conflicts between competing authorities, and conflicts for world resources but each conflict will move back to the stability of the urban-universal pattern of living.

Notes: Chapter 2

1. Bert F. Hoselitz, *A Readers Guide to the Social Sciences* (Glencoe, Ill., The Free Press, 1959). A good summary work by leaders in the various fields. It traces the social sciences back some two hundred years but establishes the specific fields on a formal educational basis essentially in the twentieth century, especially in the United States. The study of economics is dated with Alfred Marshall's *Principles of Economics*, 1890; scientific history with Leopold von Ranke's *History of the Popes*, 1912; Sociology with W. I. Thomas and Florian Znaniecki's *The Polish Peasant In Europe and America*, 1918–20; Political Science with Charles Merriam's *New Aspects of Politics;* and Psychology with J. B. Watson's *Behaviorism*, 1925. Undoubtedly, there is controversy over the significance of any of these starting dates and no defense is made over any of these books except their significance in lifting those areas to acceptance of formal and legitimate studies in American Universities.

3. THE BEGINNING OF THE
LAST REVOLUTION

i. *Origins of Urbanization*

One of the major reasons why the permanent revolution idea tends to sustain itself is due to our misjudgment as to when it began. If the revolution began five thousand years ago as some of the most respected scholars indicate, then there is no question that our revolution is at least relatively permanent. However, if it really began in the lifetime of some of the people still alive today, it is conceivable that an end may be in sight.

The basic authoritative explanation is that the physical side, the "urban" part began about five thousand years ago. Gordon Childe, an anthropologist who usually gets the credit for doing the basic research and identification of this period by the current users of the term, initiates this revolution with the following:

And so by 3000 B.C. the archaeologist's picture of Egypt, Mesopotamia, and Indus valley no longer focuses attention on communities of simple farmers, but on States embracing various professions and classes. The foreground is occupied by priests, princes, scribes, and officials, and an army of specialized craftsmen, professional soldiers, and miscellaneous laborers, all withdrawn from the primary task of food-production. . . . Priests, officials, merchants, artisans, and soldiers should represent new classes that, as classes, could find no livelihood in self-sufficient food-producing community, still less in a band of hunters. And the archaeological evidence alone suffices to confirm that expectation. The new cities are spatially larger and can accommodate a much denser population than the agricultural villages that have been absorbed in them or that still subsist beside them.[1]

Moving away from the simple urban center identified by Childe to the "Polis" that another great scholar of the city, Lewis Mumford, identifies as the origin of our modern city, we still are left with this revolution occurring about 2,500 years ago.[2] There is no intent to dispute either Childe or Mumford about the fact of the emergence of a new type of human organization in 3000 B.C. or in 700 B.C. They can even be labeled revolutions. The only point in question here is whether the rapid agglomerations, collectivities, megalopoli of the past hundred years are a "new" revolution—and more fundamental than the earlier ones described. There are many authorities that identify this revolution as occurring recently, and Lewis Mumford is among them even though he sees the present one as more of a threat and aberration than as the basis for new civilization. Before there can be any agreement on any approximate date on which the present urban-universal revolution really began we need to be more exact about its content in both its physical and mental aspects.

Our present revolution in its most visible physical aspect is the great agglomeration of peoples into urban areas, especially the forty million megalopolis of the northeastern seaboard of the United States. It is, secondly, the piling up of reinforced concrete a hundred stories high. Thirdly, it is thousands of miles of motor highways throughout the urbanized countries like the United States and western Europe. Along these highways move a long chain of metal containers which can transport the entire population at one time and a good deal of their personal belongings. The physical revolution is evident in the housing of stone, brick and concrete which can easily last a hundred or several hundreds of years. Finally, it must be the billions of dollars' worth of household goods that go into making these homes comfortable. A great deal of our productivity will be around for a long time to come, dictating the rest of the innovation.

ii. *Origins of a Universal Mentality*

The mental aspect of this recent revolution is the universalization of our beliefs and values. We are really Kantian in this respect. Our intellectual rationale demands that we think and act as if the whole universe would be expected to understand and judge us. This behavior implies that we must be more objective and less subjective in our actions since subjectivity makes communication that much more difficult. Thus, this objective communication is the foundation for what we call science and its language.

The term "universal" outlook rather than "scientific" is to be here applied. While a scientific designation might be more quickly acceptable as being more representative and more important in determining the nature of our world today, it is not sufficiently descriptive and inclusive to convey the new revolution.[3] The term "universal" can more readily describe not only the content but also the direction of the new order.

The central aspect of science which is specialization and objective communication is the very *raison d'etre* of the new urbanization taking place. But science has difficulty in handling its offshoots as legitimate attachments. Universalization of thought, on the other hand, accepts the product of science like technology of rapid communication and transportation which do not respect national boundaries. Science generally separates itself from technology. Universal also best symbolizes the drastic change which semantics has made in changing our thought processes from the limited provincial dialects that dominated our thoughts and behavior before urbanization. This emphasis on a general objective language found in the city may be thought of as a product of the scientific mentality or a product of international communication and urbanization. Or, if one prefers, it may be considered as an independent creation of men like Korzybski, Ogden, Richards, etc. In any case, it is more than empirical science.[4]

The intergroup and international contact provided by the universal outlook put a high premium on communication that went far beyond the ideolectic, i.e., that communication which is informal and usually limited to a certain area. Thus, this communication takes place more readily through mathematics, physics, chemistry and the provincial languages that have gone through semantic explication than through the local idiom. Science, of course, has certain other characteristics, such as an emphasis on empirical experimentation and verification which are integral to science alone. It has generated new discovery and it has been very influential in conditioning the nature of values which are being universalized. In a sense it has made our relationships with each other and with groups more scientific. But it is more meaningful to start the description of our times with the universal connotation than that of science because of its more encompassing scope. More will be said about this in the following chapters. Our problem here is to assess as accurately as possible when this urban-universal—and scientific, if you will—revolution really began.

iii. *Explanation for False Dating*

The starting point in arriving at a meaningful analysis of the present urban civilization in the United States or in England must be to pinpoint its genesis at approximately the first quarter of the nineteenth century. Using the framework already described, the ancient urbanization had no real bearing on present urbanization.

Little attention will be given to the so-called ancient cities, and early polis, because there seems to have been a tendency to overvalue the city in history. The main reason for that is due to its being the nucleus for the future; it had the future in its very being. Another reason for the overvaluation of the early city in history has been its role as a depository of the written records which are used in the study of the past. These records, being written primarily by residents of the city, emphasize the personalities of the city more than the "folk" of the country. Thus, a false perspective is given of the fundamental organization of life at that period of time. It is strange that this should be done after so much attention is placed by all anthropologists and historians on the transition from the hunter, gatherer, fisher economies and civilizations to man the cultivator of the soil, irrigator of land, domesticator of animals, which is now identified as the coming of the Neolithic revolution. This revolution receives comparatively little attention when compared to the study of the cities in their midst. It is as though civilization passed from the primitive hunter-collector to the twentieth-century specialist on an automotive production line without the seven thousand years of essentially agriculturally based civilizations.

A part of this neglect of stability is again due to the overemphasis of the present by the social sciences earlier and past. These terms are only constructs but they are suggested.[5] Take, for example, the folk-urban category of "ideal" types used so frequently to interpret the present widely used by anthropologists, sociologists and historians, who are encouraged to see the sharp differences thus multiplying the perspective of change. There is no full agreement on what should or should not be included in the definition and explication of these terms, but with modification they remain in general use. Thus, in order for the social scientist to fit all social groups into a continuum, from primitive folk units like the Yucatan into sharp contrast with present-day Chicago urbanism, seven thousand years of a relatively stable and distinct agriculturally based civilization like China is put into a stage of transition. Why not an "ideal" type of agricultural-provincial society? Should this be done, stability would be emphasized rather than change.

iv. *Two Examples of Confusion: China and Rome*[6]

China managed to develop a high level of civilization of long duration that cannot be put into the "folk" construct, especially if the most authoritative one, Robert Redfield's, is used. His ideal folk community is small—one where the people in it can come to know each other. The Chinese civilization has its basis in the family, but the people feel part of a great empire, the Middle Kingdom. Redfield's folk community is isolated. The Chinese are in touch with the civilization of centuries through the residence among them of scholars. The Chinese have a written language and books which are not, by definition, characteristic of the folk. There are, of course, aspects of the folk society which can apply to China but they are not dominant.

Nor can the Chinese civilization be put in the urban construct. The population of agricultural-provincial China is not of sufficient density as are modern cities. They do not have the high degree of specialization, nor the segmentation of roles. The social relationships are not of the transitory level as the present urban. But as with the folk construct there are certain characteristics which apply, however, at the expense of appreciating the agri-provincial civilization of China.

The civilization of classical Rome which lasted nearly a thousand years is also misjudged by the above constructs. It is neither truly folk nor urban. It had certain density, literacy and specialization. But it is more realistically viewed as a large center for adjusting rural problems. Rome's civilization was built on its service to the agri-provincial civilization. It provided an administration set-up to deal with the problems of expanding populations. The independent small land-owning farmer emergence of land holding and cultivation never was feasible as a self-executing method even when protection was assured. The prolific procreation of the farm population which is associated with agricultural families nearly always meant a division of land—with resulting conflict between the children. Even with primogeniture it always meant finding new land for the rest of the children. And with population expanding increasingly this could only be done by displacing others. Thus administrative Rome had to perform the difficult task of all kinds of resettlement.

Rome had also to provide the difficult responsibility of dealing with the problems of soil exhaustion. This is one of the perennial problems of agri-provincial civilizations. China was able to solve it by her method of fertilization of the soil. But Rome, possibly because of the poorer soil, was forced to rely increasingly for its wheat on supplies outside of Italy. One of the reasons for these increased demands was the increased population of Rome, but another had been the exhaustion of the soil, especially in the South Latium district. The land could still be utilized for vineyards which provided a good product for trade, but it also made Rome more vulnerable to the vagaries of trade balance and the guarantee of secure delivery could never be assured.

Rome's activities were ninety-five percent for the rural areas, and when she could not perform them the rural village could withdraw to provide a subsistence economy for itself or look for another city that might do it. The city of the agri-provincial civilization was intrinsically a part of it and failed when it could not perform its agricultural functions. The urban community of the twentieth century exists essentially for other cities. The small farmer now is the parasite and rapidly disappearing.

The agri-provincial revolution hitherto discussed reached points of stability in the dominant places of the world from around 5000 B.C. in areas like China, India, and along the Mediterranean, and eventually in Europe great and stable civilizations developed. The essence of this type of civilization was to marry specific people to a specific area of land. The word marriage can hardly be strong enough; it was biologically to link man to the land as the fish is a captive of water, or an animal of its skin. This type of marriage to the land is well illustrated in the recent period by the serf in Russia before emancipation in 1861, or the free tenant and peasant in China before 1911. In countries with serfdom one did not ordinarily purchase land without also buying the people on it; they came with the land. The free tenant, peasant or farmer inherited or purchased his land. Directly or indirectly they all had to pay constantly for legal and military people who helped protect from outsiders or provide courts to settle disputes between competing inheritors.

The peasant certainly relied on a primitive form of "collectivity" known as a city, but it was fundamentally different from the urban-universal city of the latter nineteenth century. The early collectivities were in reality islands in a "sea of agriculture." They depended on the peasant and their primary service was designed for the peasants. They were temple cities, military garrisons, exchange centers or all combined. These "service" people naturally developed a rationale for themselves to remove them from the parasitic category.

The agri-provincial based city was not the modern city of an urbanized country where the great majority of the products produced are for the residents of other cities. The resident of the pre-nineteenth-century city still had the mode of thought of the provincials, their mode of transport. He was productive of goods or services primarily for the provincial since the overwhelming majority of people in his time were those who worked the land. The urbanized numbers in countries like the United States and England have reversed the urban-rural scale. We now have over 90 percent of the people as nonfarmers, thus the whole mental framework of the base of production is therefore altered.

The Athenses, Spartas, Alexandrias and Romes of that day thought of themselves and their skills, especially the intellectual and military, as being the source of life while the peasants were therefore less than human. Being better organized than the peasants and maintaining the records they managed to convince themselves and future generations of this. The good life according to the Athenian was to be a citizen-politician; or for the Spartan, the soldier. Alexandria, because of its high need for geological records to protect the farmer, was to emphasize the astronomer, and Rome the administrator. All of these were nevertheless "service" functions to the peasants, the serfs, and slaves.

v. Stability of Traditional Society

There was a great deal of stability in the peasant's life. We lose sight of this because historically we tend to concentrate on the cities which left the records. We believe that the removal of one family for another tended to be a fundamental change in the history of man. It would be as though in looking at American presidential elections every four years one would conclude the nation to have gone through fundamental political changes. It would only be true if one began with the fortunes of given personalities rather than the organization of our entire society.

We have a great deal still to learn from countries like China and India where agricultural civilizations did not lose sight of their foundations and developed more rational bases of organization adjusted to agriculture. They survived for thousands of years with minimum conflict. The instabilities and conflicts in Western civilization are treated as more important since it was not the conflict that was father to the new basis for man's life, but rather the poorer European soil and expanding population that put a premium on a service that would obtain the agricultural products from more productive regions of the world. Thus commerce and discovery of new lands permitted collectivities of the size of New Amsterdam, London, Bristol, etc.[7]

The basis then for the present urban-universal revolution was the expansion of peasantry to the point that mankind faced the challenge of limiting its population growth through war, or some organizational basis which would prevent the expansion of population. Since the population was not organized on a world scale, the practice of birth control by any one group simply eliminated itself from competition by its neighbors, and encouraged eventual destruction or enslavement. While war, on the other hand, had always been a population stabilizer it was so haphazard and contrary to the intelligence of man that as soon as urbanism was able to handle large populations this became the predominant way of settling the excess population. The modern city has traditionally been a consumer of populations rather than a producer. And while urbanism will face challenges to instability from many areas, it is not likely to be from overpopulation.

Notes: Chapter 3

1. V. Gordon Childe, *Man Makes Himself* (Mentor, 1961), p. 115. Originally published in 1936.
2. Lewis Mumford, *The City in History* (New York, Harcourt, Brace & World, Inc., 1961), p. 72.
3. Using the "universe" as a more general concept than "science" I take from Hannah Arendt's work *The Human Condition* (New York, Doubleday-Anchor, 1959), pp. 225–239. Miss Arendt's

works are in many respects the genesis of many of the ideas presented in this book. At one point (pp. 244–246) Miss Arendt dates this revolution. She points out that it is only in the past few decades that we have begun to live in a world where truth is derived from the cosmic and universal as distinguished from the terrestrial and natural laws. She also maintains that "universal" has acquired a very specific meaning "valid beyond our solar system."

4. While Alfred Korzybski pioneered a change in our language processes in his work *Science and Sanity*, Stuart Chase in his *Power of Words* (New York, Harcourt & Brace, 1953) capably communicates this lingual change and the role of people like Korzybski.

5. *The Primitive World and Its Transformations* by Robert Redfield (Ithaca, N.Y., Cornell University Press, 1953) is truly one of the great scholarly works on this subject. Yet the emphasis of this book, which is obvious from the title, is upon revolution and change rather than the value of stability.

6. The material on Rome, China and agriculture comes primarily from Crane Brinton's *A History of Civilization* and Norman Grass, *A History of Agriculture*.

7. Adam Smith in his *Wealth of Nations*, Modern Library Series, p. 379, had observed the distinctiveness of the coastal cities like London and Bristol from inland cities like Paris where the dependency was on the surrounding agricultural area, these coastal cities were still not modern. They mastered space through shipping but their function was still primarily for a rural civilization.

4. "THE NEW ORDER OF THE AGES"

The urban-universal civilization manifesting itself most extensively in North America and Western Europe today is both a physical condition and a mental outlook. It is becoming as harmoniously wedded and interrelated as the previous agri-provincial civilization. Its fabric and pattern are already well defined; its form is less apparent, but no longer obscure. There are two books to which the author is greatly indebted for the intellectual genesis of this chapter. Hence it is appropriate that the reader be aware of them at the inception since their impact is much more important than any specific reference that might be made to them. The first is Jean Gottmann's *Megalopolis*, 1961, which optimistically describes the new emerging urbanism.[1] The second is Hannah Arendt's *The Human Condition*, 1958, which somewhat pessimistically describes our emerging mental outlook of the rise of society, and the loss of potency for man to act as man.[2]

The main point of this chapter is to explicate the concept urban-universal, and separate it from other terms and connotations so that a specific referent of the present condition might be made. Our language describing the present itself creates the greatest obstacle to an understanding of what is happening. For purposes of clarity, attention will be given to the first half of the term urban-universal. It connotes a more physical and tangible characterization of the present condition. After this we will direct the attention to the latter half and more abstract part of the urban-universal concept. Urban will then be treated as our means and Universal as the end of our action. Universal as an end provides a clear projection of the urban characteristic. While the analysis of these terms may seem somewhat extensive, it is one without which the reader cannot appreciate the emerging condition.

i. *Urbanism as a Physical Phenomenon*

The term "urban" juxtaposes itself against the term rural and therefore means those things the rural is not. It means a density of people that survive in non-agricultural pursuits. There may be an integrity to it as is often true in older cities, or the city or collectivity may be without any overriding unity. Let us first explore the term in its most physical aspect, i.e., population densities of non-agriculturally employed peoples. This is a clear, meaningful yardstick for comparison of population collectivities the world over. It also has significance for separating the feudal agricultural period from the modern, industrial period. If we look at the world historically we find that prior to 1800 no unified collectivity of people could contain over a million people, and in only a few exceptional cases were there groups of more than 25,000. The urban areas, or the megalopolis of the twentieth century, finds a mushroom type of growth of many large cities. In 1960, there were 112 cities in the world with over one million population. Their total population was 285 million and constituted nearly ten percent of the world population. If we lower the figure to 100,000 we find that cities in 1960 contained over a third of the world's population.[3] The measurement that Gottman uses to indicate the future trend is to class the whole northeastern seaboard of the United States in the category of a single urbanized area, contiguous, and in constant touch, with relatively common problems. Another, though smaller, is around the Chicago area, and a third is in the California area. These constitute population densities never found in the agri-provincial world. Thus they serve as a good contrast between the new and the old.

The problem with the population density yardstick is that it begins to lose its measurement value when we get into the mid-twentieth century world. Cities, prior to the mid-nineteenth century, presented boundaries and populations distinct from the rural. Now in some countries like Britain and the United States the rural, for all practical purposes, has disappeared. For if cities are not to be examined in any other way than nonfarming population per square mile, whole nations could now be classed as one urbanized area. With hardly more than five percent engaged in farming plus the conquest of space through rapid transportation and communication, nearly the whole United States and England have become, and perform, the same social, political and economical functions that were ordinarily associated with city life. Urbanization thus must be contrasted with the rural in its consequences on social organization if we are to realize what urbanization means to us today.

ii. *Urbanism as a Social Relationship*

The classical formula for recognizing the urbanite by characteristics other than physical proximity was formulated by Louis Wirth in 1938 in an article published in

THE AMERICAN JOURNAL OF SOCIOLOGY. A section of the abstract of the article sums up Wirth's definition:

> . . . For sociological purposes a city is a relatively large, dense, and permanent settlement of heterogeneous individuals. Large numbers account for individual variability, the relative absence of intimate personal acquaintanceship, the segmentalization of human relations which are largely anonymous, superficial, and transitory, and associated characteristics. Density involves diversification and specialization, the coincidence of close physical contact and distant social relations . . . heterogeneity tends to break down rigid social structures and to produce increased mobility, instability, and insecurity. . . . The pecuniary nexus tends to displace personal relations, and institutions tend to cater to mass rather than to individual requirements. The individual thus becomes effective only as he acts through organized groups.[4]

iii. *Urbanism as a Master of Space*

Wirth's description of urbanism has been more fruitful in explaining what was transpiring to man in the city than the simple density statistics. And it was probably accurate for the time that he looked at urban life. But his emphasis on the city as the universe, its instability and insecurity as contrasted to the rural no longer is applicable. The city social structure is being increasingly drawn closer together—not, however, within the narrow confines of the city, but by a national orientation, and a class structure based on profession and merit. Driven by the mass media of communication, of economical efficiency that comes from scale, the urban community is becoming physically rationalized, and socially more disciplined and more organized on a national scale than it ever was on the local. The anonymity and the alienation of the individual in the city of the nineteenth century is rapidly disappearing, and furthermore, the traditional functions of the city dweller for the country are gone. The national, in fact, universally oriented urban areas in countries like the United States now identify themselves more readily in national or universal aspects. There is little memory or consciousness of man as a provincial, bound to a local identity.

While anonymity and alienation was the lot of the urbanite in the late nineteenth and early twentieth century, groupism and community are the predominant characteristics of the highly urbanized countries in the latter half of the twentieth century. Whereas the liberal philosophy was the *sine qua non* of the period of the revolution, socialism, status quo and balance are the cries of the crowd that calls for an end to Revolution.

iv. *Fear of the New Urbanism*

As might be expected with the emergence of a new order there was a dreadful fear of it, especially by those most sensitive of what was occurring in the world. Some of the most poetic statements were also made on behalf of the few who found the period of revolution exhilarating. They tried to glamorize the individual in a world of rapid change and draw a gloomy picture of any stability, past or future. Fear of this new urbanism is best viewed by looking at some recent books which tried to idealize the process of change and revolution by trying to give the individual dignity and meaning in the world of change even when they foresaw the coming of the new age which they dreaded.

One of the earliest and perhaps the most profound prognosticators of this new urban-universal civilization was Ortega y Gasset in a book first published in 1930, *The Revolt of the Masses*. He feared that the coming great agglomerations of people who will be born to a life of plenty, with conveniences and security, and all life's advantages will be little more than urban slaves committed to some national leader and doctrine.[5]

Twenty years later Ortega's thesis regarding the decline of the free individual was picked up and demonstrated with empirical evidence by a team of researchers led by David Riesman in the provocative book, *The Lonely Crowd*. Here once again the authors were unhappy because the evidence in America indicated that the present period, which is characterized by an age of consumption rather than production, and an incipient population decline, manifested itself in a crowd culture which was "other-directed," and losing the power of creativity, innovation and individuality.[6] Six years later a sensationally popular and scholarly book by William H. Whyte, Jr., *The Organization Man*, gave a sharper picture of this same trend.[7] Just as Riesman, Whyte found in the mid-twentieth century that we began to subscribe to a new ethic, the "social ethic" which went beyond the local boundaries. He contrasted it against our nineteenth century "Protestant ethic," which had the goal of individual creativity against the twentieth century organizational projection which expands into an unlimited Leviathan of national socialization.

The fourth of these social critics apprehensive of the agglomerated urbanized masses, the one already mentioned at the beginning of this chapter, Hannah Arendt, is perhaps the most vehement in her criticism of the social ethic. "The modern age," she says, "which began with such promise may end in the deadliest, most sterile passivity history has ever known."[8]

These writings exemplify a fear that these critics of the urbanized organization had, not so much that there won't be a few of them around, but that their ideal of the world where the individual could stand firm in a world of change was becoming a romantic myth. It disgusted them to think that the individual began to prefer the security of the mass and the involvement of some national conformity rather than the anxiety of living in a world of the unexpected. There is no criticism meant here of these heroic visionaries and defenders of the "permanent Revolution." Two points, however, need to be made. One, that twentieth-century urbanism has rejected their concept of the good life. The nonconforming, ever hungry for change, individual makes a romantic, superman type of figure but not one that will be used for emulation. When given a choice human nature is most likely to be conservative about change. The second point is that life can also be lived meaningfully and heroically in a society of stability as it was for a few in revolution. The consequence of this increased socialization is naturally a greater conformity, a decrease of individuality and independence. Thus the main characteristic of the new city with the "social ethic" becomes interdependence, and the individual recognizes himself as a part of the group and attempts to be effective through the group.

This increased groupism is evident by the popular political choices toward social welfare that have been made since World War II in western nations. It goes, however, far beyond the larger and more formal groupings to a great variety of informal national groups which spring up for every occasion of social conflict. It was de Tocqueville who first observed that Americans organize a committee or an association for every undertaking. This socialization, as de Tocqueville recognized, was the true harbinger of the developing nations.

These associations from the professional to the service organizations are now becoming the surrogates for the previous attachments and loyalties that commanded our actions on a local level. There has been a phenomenal growth in physical and social mobility by the industrialized populations which feel themselves more subject to national or world action than to the locale in which they reside. Here, however, we must be careful not to confuse activity with change. Certainly every physical move from city to city brings a considerable private excitement for the individual, new friends, new physical phenomena, but the basic national and world pattern of urbanism remains to provide continuity and stability to our behavior. Nor does a merit type of social mobility provide many discontinuities so long as the individual is selected early in life and acculturated according to the profession for which he is fitted. Most crucial in providing this stability is the extensive biographic document on prior performance, tax and credit record, medical record, court record, plus increased other vital statistics which provides an identity and surveillance as extensive as the agri-provincial society ever gave. Gone is the anonymity of the transitional urbanism of the late nineteenth and early twentieth century in American and Western Europe. Gone also is individualism and anxiety most associated with that transitional period.

v. *Records and Social Control in the New Urbanism**

The specific and most important characteristic fostered by urbanism towards stability, however, has been the multiplication of information, data, record-keeping on all industrial productivity, but for our purposes especially on each individual. Louis Wirth was not aware of this factor in urban living since it is only now becoming a conspicuous concomitant of the new urbanism. The freedom that the city in revolutionary times gave to the individual who broke from old social ties in the provincial area provided for a good deal more restlessness and change in the city. Records supplemented by the rapid communication media which put one at a dial's turn from an inquisitor are becoming as strong a restraint and control as any family, church or small village could impose on the individual before. They are making anonymity and anxiety in the city a thing of the past.

This phenomenon, the accumulation of records on all phases of human activity of all people now being born in an industrial nation, is perhaps a unique and one of the most pervasive social controls of the twentieth century. Records of the nature already cited, reduced to formulas on standardized IBM cards are reaching a geometric rate of progression. Like the machine with interchangeable parts, facts on the individual American can be transferred in minutes from the credit bureau to the bank, to the new charge account, to the tax office, to the police station, to the researcher, etc. Our dossiers expand and multiply.

This recording is not the result of any sinister plan to spy on people, deprive them of their privacy, or satisfy some morbid human curiosity, and this is why our awareness of their significance may escape us. The accumulation

* This section published in *Social Science Journal.*

of records is a product of our urbanization and mobility, of the level of industrialization and mechanization of production. Records are important in economizing resources, in facilitating activity in a highly mobile system. The complex network of records on humans which are located in every industrial nation draw together the activity of millions of people into some order for political and social order, for production, distribution and allocation of goods and values. Without such records, a nation the size of the United States would end in chaos in a relatively short period of time, and so we tend only to see their benevolence.

Primitive societies were able to carry on their activity for livelihood without records. But they were forced to limit their social organization to an order which grew out of face-to-face relationships and were doomed to remain at that level as long as they failed to use records. A claim to a piece of property in a primitive society could not extend beyond the physical possession of it. While in an industrial nation it is not unusual to own property without ever seeing it. Most of the activity of industrial countries is bound up in its objective records. This is probably more true in the United States than any other country because of our size and degree of urbanization.

One is then faced with the question of the uniqueness of this new condition. Did people not possess records in the past? Certainly there were records in the society of ancient Greece and Rome, as well as in the intervening years since. There are government records of taxes, church records, and military records. All of these combined were still a meager source of information on the behavior of individuals. There were a few exceptions. These were the records on individuals who were the kings, princes and great military leaders located in cities. Their actions were often reported in minute detail. And their lives, whether they realized it or not, were to a certain extent circumscribed by these records. The great majority even of the urbanized, however, never found their lives significant enough to be available for public record. Today, however, the treatment of extensive recording that was once reserved for kings is regular practice for all of us. A brief examination of the extent of these records on all of us will indicate the degree to which we are being rapidly circumscribed by the marks left of our past activities.

The government of an industrial nation is one of the main collectors and depositories of individual records. Through birth certificates and passports, these governments establish membership from nonmembership in the nation. There are extensive sets of records in industrial countries on all types of material wealth, and in whose possession this wealth is located. Real estate, automobiles, airplanes, animals, etc., are registered with the government. Through tax policies, and especially the income tax, a substantial amount of the rest of an individual's wealth is recorded. Police and court records will indicate the activity of those who have come into conflict over property and personal relations. A further profile of an individual's relationship to the social order can be obtained from public educational facilities, public welfare records, health department records, fire department, etc. The foregoing list by no means exhausts the sources of official recording.

A second vital source of record deposition would be in the nonofficial category. This second source is far more important in the United States than in countries where the government is more actively involved in the nation's business. Newspaper offices are virtual treasuries of vital information on people. The information from these files is often accessible to the general public. Business establishments are in the forefront of the activity of recording transfers of wealth, and have national bureaus that can, in minutes, give indication of an individual's credit rating. Hospitals, doctors, lawyers, and countless other professional categories have vital information which permit that delicate web of interrelationships to function in the complex industrial society. This nonofficial area of record-keeping is more difficult to locate and assess but, through standardized forms and methods, is becoming susceptible to rapid means of information interchange.

A third source of records—those gathered by the professional and "disinterested" researcher—merits special consideration. These records could be put in the above category but the motivation of this group is different from the above. This group claims from science its authority to examine and further record. Its interest is to provide studies for analysis, comparison and generalization of their findings. In order to do this, the researcher cannot avoid coming across vital personal information. E. A. Shils deals with the ethics of this group in his essay "Social Inquiry and the Autonomy of the Individual."[9] An indication of the personal information which can be published is available in *Men at the Top* by Eliott Osborn.[10] Comparative analysis, sparked by curiosity, in the name of science, is an explanation for a considerable amount of research in this area. Robert Wernick, in his book *They've Got Your Number,* indicates the continual availability of certain studies on specific individuals. He cites one case in Minnesota where a study had been made a generation earlier on scores of infants. This study was later followed up on this same group when they were adults.[11]

The value to social science of studies of this nature is easily defended. Yet it is apparent that an increase of this type of study tends to make more extensive information available on the lives of these people. The social science researcher is probably, in most cases, concerned with the ethics of the way in which such information is attained and made available, but there is no agreed code on this research, even though there would be certain legal restrictions on publication. Once again, it is not the certain use of these records which is being examined but the very existence of them, their potential, and their number.

One thing that the social scientist unwittingly contributes to, in addition to greater availability of these records, is that they are being drawn together from many sources and correlated. The police, of course, especially the FBI, have used and developed such methods to further expedite their duties, but the FBI is usually limited to certain categories of people whereas the researcher examines the whole gamut, and is perhaps more interested in the normal than the abnormal. The point to be drawn from this third category is that there is a conscious effort at drawing together this information without any intent they do. Since our society, because of its size and mobility of influencing the recordee's behavior, although in fact and the desire for efficiency, is learning to rely more on the record than on a personal interview, the social scientist with his skill and ability is there to provide this efficiency. It is conceivable that a standardized cumulative record file on each one of us will be the basis on which our next job or entrance into a social organization will depend. The record will be in the possession of some official agency. And it will all begin as it has already begun through voluntary commitment and unconcerned objective accumulation. (Our future applications will be, "Please forward my file to . . .")

vi. *Two Terms That Confuse*

An explanation must be given why two more customary terms associated with the modern civilization are not as fitting as the term "universal." The first of the two is the word "industry." We see it so commonly used in historical studies beginning with the sixteenth century that an explanation is necessary if we fail to use it. Every school child has learned of the "Industrial Revolution," a second, and even a third industrial revolution. We tend to associate a theory of progress with it, and list every non-agricultural invention as a sign of it. It takes in the compass and the astrolabe, printing and mapmaking, and from steam power to atomic energy. The mechanization of agriculture is sometimes lumped under it as well, though most technical improvements in crop and animal husbandry are labeled under a separate concept, the "agricultural revolution."

While the term industrial has merit in its use to describe a period, there are corresponding difficulties. The greatest difficulty with the term is its reference to action, to doing something. Thus, even without the adjunct "revolution" behind it there is an impression of change. And if we are to examine the evidence of stability the term would have to be separated from its traditional understanding, which would be no small task in keeping things straight. Perhaps an even greater difficulty with

using the concept of industry for description is well stated
by Raymond Aron in the book *World Technology and
Human Destiny:*

> . . . even if we assume that industrial society such as we
> know it has generally spread throughout the world, we
> still have no clear picture as to what man, using this
> society as a point of departure, will do with his life,
> what he would like to do with his life.
> . . . industrial society is no more than the collection of
> means necessary to provide the majority of people with
> decent material living conditions.[12]

Thus it loses its utility if we ask where is "industry" taking
us? Will industry level off, continue at the same rate, or
increase in its rate of development, and with what social
order?

The last two questions also apply to another widely
associated term with our modern civilization, the concept
of "science." We are also accustomed to referring to our
period as an "age of science," and we credit a great deal
of our present accomplishments to scientists. All this is
obviously true, and while the designation might appear
more logical and certainly more recognizable, it would
also be a misleading use of the term. First, as most active
scientists will admit, science does not dictate a social order.
A philosopher like Burtt may think he sees in it the assumptions of science, or at least the work of scientists,
especially in the desire to predict and control. But this
still does not spell out any specific end, and while scientists
may try to control some forces, especially relevant to
human affairs, these ideals will be based on grounds other
than scientific. Science is neutral about the social order
even if scientists and the social order are not neutral
about science.

A good indication of the subordination of science to a social order is apparent to what has happened to science in the past few decades. Science until then was based on, and subordinated to, a natural, terrestrial end. Since Einstein science has been transferred in its base and its productivity to an abstract universal outlook, thus changing the ends and base to which science is being used. We can use the scientific method more extensively toward certain goals, but the employment of a scientist to find a cure for cancer does not make health the end of science. Nor does the creation of an atomic bomb make destruction an end of science. Nor does the search for universal truths make science more scientific than the search for natural truths. Thus to think of ourselves as a scientific world or order does not distinguish between a pursuit of health or destruction, and do any justice to the term science. Hence while we revere the term today it falls short of describing and predicting the order that is developing, the universal order.

vii. *Urbanism Becomes Universal*

The pursuit of things "universal" is the goal supreme today, it is the new "truth."[13] The one who knows the universal language, mathematics, speaks the language of the future. Those on the side of universal manhood suffrage, the Universal Declaration of Human Rights, writing of history from an international base, organizers of religious dogma from a universal base, founders of organizations with universal outlook are on the side of the inheritors of the new truth. The central designation that is meant here is that universal implies a unified system for every intelligent being here on earth and it is a goal that is rapidly being approached. It will not mean an equalitarian order, but it will mean one that will consider consequences of action in terms of an anonymous, abstract, world public, rather than in reference to a specific private and concrete reality. When a choice is to be made between a private personal gain and the abstract "public good" the latter will be the yardstick. It is interesting to see how this universal outlook has already affected the newly developed parts of the world. R. P. Dore in his very scholarly study of *City Life in Japan* shows how drastically the universalistic outlook has affected Japan. Japan had a long tradition of loyalty to the family, or of loyalty to another person. A nationwide poll conducted in 1953 regarding loyalty to the family, revealed a startling change which had taken place in this respect. On a question that asked the following:

> Someone to whom you are indebted for past favors has a son who takes the entrance examination for a certain firm. A representative of the firm calls to ask you for a personal opinion of the son's qualities. You happen to know that he is an unreliable person. How would you answer . . .[14]

Only 23 percent said they would do their best to get the son accepted by the firm, while 48 percent said they would tell the truth about him.

The Universal outlook is a frame of mind which means the pursuit of an abstract public truth rather than a specific and concrete private reality. It means equality of opportunity and the concept of justice that grows out of this. Universal means a generalized and unified view of the world; it means universities, or seats of learning that have united many vocations and philosophies under one order.

It is a small wonder that the "new universal" outlook appears to be such a threat to traditional privacy. This universal outlook makes a person's illness no longer a private affair—it is open to criticism and review by everyone in the world, especially if it is contagious. A person's unemployment is not a private affair any longer, but a concern of the whole world since it apparently influences the entire world. It took the United States some time to accept the fact that unemployment in the United States was a domestic affair. It is taking the entire world some time to realize that the production and explosion of atomic weapons is not an internal affair of a nation. And with our great concern of overpopulation, every woman's pregnancy becomes a concern for all. What the universal dictates is to deal with the individual and group problems not at the private, small group or fragmented level, but to solve them, or at least give the guiding principles to their solution, at the universal level. The universal outlook will, of course, become restrictive on science and technology. It will direct what will be studied and to what ends it will be used. The investment that will be put into innovation will undoubtedly be limited to its compatibility with a universal social order which inherently would have its own preservation as the primary goal.

Let us look more closely now at the developing urban-universal order, the things that will be dictated by this order. It is above all a world order, which physically, economically and intellectually imposes itself on the world without political power. Its greatest force is publicity, with corresponding public approbation or disapproval, which can be exposed to the world in a few minutes. We are rapidly becoming aware of this new order, and although we might like to restrain it we feel helpless to do so. The communication may be about the assassination of a President of the United States or the change of administration in the Soviet Union; it may be on far less significant matters like a new style from Paris, a riot in Tokyo, but in minutes these become universal matters, affecting all people and therefore will inevitably be put under a social control like the U.N. which can act for the world. A fad like rock and roll is no longer limited in space and time; it is instantaneous all over the world.

Such a wide communication of ideas would seem to be a prelude to faster change but that is not the case. Just as the speed of communication has increased, the method itself becomes more standardized and fixed, and the products of communication flow in decreasing variation. Where the youngsters of the world forty years ago learned and preserved a variety of local custom dances, today they all do one, whether in Tokyo, London, Caracas or San Francisco. De Tocqueville called attention to this phenomenon of uniformity over a hundred years ago in his *Democracy in America*. While he observed that the United States was one of the largest organized and centralized civilizations, he found that it already possessed an unusual amount of uniformity.

The emulation of peoples with regard to such matters as dance and music is of the most voluntaristic types, i.e., no one has to adopt it for survival. And still the tendency toward uniformity is high. What of products and behavior that are necessary to survival like those regarding atomic energy? How much chance is there for variety in international radio and telivision channels? An early universal accomplishment will be universal television for instantaneous viewing of occurrences throughout the world. How much innovation will there be with such visibility?

Notes: Chapter 4

1. Jean Gottman, *Megalopolis*, New York, The Twentieth Century Fund, 1961.
2. Hannah Arendt, *The Human Condition*, Garden City, New York, Doubleday Anchor, 1959.
3. Frederick J. Osborn and Arnold Whittich, *The New Towns*, New York, McGraw Hill, 1963, p. 31.
4. Louis Wirth, "Urbanism as a Way of Life," *The American Journal of Sociology*, July, 1938.
5. Ortega y Gasset, *The Revolt of the Masses*, New York, W. W. Norton, 1932 (See Chapters 4 and 13).
6. David Riesman, et. al., *The Lonely Crowd*, New York, Doubleday Anchor, 1950.
7. William H. Whyte, Jr., *The Organization Man*, New York, Simon & Schuster, 1956.
8. Arendt, *op. cit.*, p. 295.
9. Edward A. Shils, "Social Inquiry & The Autonomy Of The Individual," Essay in *The Human Meaning Of The Social Sciences*, ed. by Daniel Lerner, New York, Meridian Books, 1959.
10. Elliot Osborn, *Men at the Top*, New York, Harper, 1959.
11. Robert Wernick, *They've Got Your Number*, New York, W. W. Norton, 1956, p. 111.
12. Raymond Aron, ed., *World Technology & Human Destiny*, Ann Arbor, Mich., University of Michigan Press, 1963, pp. 65–66.
13. Arendt, *op. cit.*, p. 225, Miss Arendt places the development of a new science which considers the nature of the earth from the viewpoint of the universe as one of the three great events of the modern age.
14. R. P. Dore, *City Life in Japan*, Berkeley, Cal., University of California Press, 1963, p. 381.

Part II
Emerging Signs of Stability

The following chapters examine the signs of leveling off of revolutionary activity. There are four areas examined: the first is the degree to which building and its de-escalating tendency manifests itself in a completed art form. The second deals with a new vital environment. The third with political authority and the fourth with a re-emergence of a class structure based essentially on a meritocracy.

5. PHYSICAL RESTRAINTS ON CHANGE IN MATURE URBANIZATION

i. *Emergence of a New Rationale Consistent with Physical Developments*

The most advanced urban societies have a unique characteristic about themselves that sharply distinguishes them from the rural societies. Their attention has been more on production than on the "good life." Indeed, if we are to accept the thesis of Max Weber in *The Protestant Ethic* or R. H. Tawney in *Religion and the Rise of Capitalism* we realize that productivity itself was the criterion of good in the New World. Any manner of living could be justified by the physical fruits of the effort. While this philosophy left a good deal to be desired, it was a good pragmatic, rule-of-thumb method for making decisions. Coming out of an order of life where shortages of food, shelter, and clothing were an accepted way of life, it presented a rational alternative—especially if life itself was to be cherished. Thus, the new found success at productivity had an intrinsic rationale for the producer even though it might conflict with the cherished values on which the old system of security was built.

The American Revolution is a prime example of a choice of productivity over order. It must be recognized that the agricultural order in America was far less applicable than in the "Old World." Scarcity of the basic resources in relation to the population was less in Colonial America than ever known by the civilized Europeans. The climate, the land, the animal resources, all were available in greater quantity than ever before—especially since they had the good fortune of being based on the most advanced technology that had been developed to that time. Equally beneficial toward increased productivity was the fact that the social order of Europe was not transported uniformly nor very successfully. Too few of the aristocracy migrated to assure the orderly functioning of the army, the church, and the government. Thus, there was insufficient assurance for the smooth flow of the European order, of the known stability. The new, makeshift order was open to question and often less stabilizing than a new indigenous frontier justice which became the symbol of the American West. The basis on which this new justice was distributed increasingly supported the producers at the expense of the old morality and the old stability based on agri-provincial order. The consequences of this was production; wealth of food, shelter, and clothing appeared in abundance justifying the violation of order and stability.

As long as there was a residue of the old European order to provide a conscience, and as long as the newly discovered methods of productivity did not overproduce in terms of demands, the system functioned as beautifully as a revolution could. Productivity as an ethic reached new heights of amorality in the period following the Civil War, not only in America but also in Europe. It also reached heights of productivity never known before—a productivity that made scarcity a thing of the past. Farmers found that they could grow more corn than man could eat. Manufacturers discovered that they could produce more clothes than man could wear, and more railroads than man could ride. The affluence grew to a degree that some tried to cultivate "waste" as a criterion for the good life. The social standards based on production, rationalized for revolution, were irreconcilable with a stable society.

The contradictions inherent in the standards developed out of productivity became painfully apparent at the time when every American was told he could have "two chickens in every pot and two cars in every garage." The revelation was even more appalling because subconsciously Americans already sensed that there could be ten chickens and ten cars, and no one desiring to consume them. We postponed that goal, or rather that nightmare for another twenty years. An artificial arrest of production followed by even more artificial demands of war kept the old standards based on production, and more production, alive. It was kept alive for another generation by turning from private affluence to public affluence. But hitherto productivity could not outrun consumption unless consumption included waste, and this eventually runs counter to man's intelligence. No amount of social manipulation could keep urbanized man to go on deceiving himself into acquisition for the sake of acquisition as an intelligent outlook. The generation of the 1960s in America and in Western Europe, to the horror of the preconditioned parents, refused to participate in what they called the "rat race" of production for status. Why eat more food than you need? Why work if production is assured without your effort? Why participate in war to waste resources? Their questions stuck in the throats of the parents who tried to give logical, scientific, economic and moral answers that had no basis in a world of surplus productivity. A new social order was already in the process of birth. It was apparent in the new monumentalism that was being produced. Human labor was gearing itself for extinction by concentration on producing a physical plant that would last a hundred or a thousand years with minimum repair. This was an emerging America sharply different from its past. It could be understood only in relationship to its past and the sharp break from it.

A world where "work" as a compulsive act to maintain life would no longer be essential is a strange and often frightening outlook. With the exception of a fortunate few in the history of mankind, who were wealthy enough to do only what they desired, the great man always had to work for their livelihood. Now, urban scientific society freed man from "work." We would actually live and have some of the amenities of life without ever working. The reader is not to mistake the freedom from work as in any way related to a desire to be freed from activity. We all want to be freed from work, i.e., doing those things we would prefer not doing, if we were compensated without being obligated to do it. For man is an animal of action who craves activity as naturally as he craves rest. The vital distinction between work and activity is the desire to do the latter even though no extrinsic reward is forthcoming. Thus we can expect to find man as active, and perhaps more active in a world without work as he was found in the world where work was necessary for survival. We will still desire a certain amount of exertion for our health physically plus an even greater amount for our satisfactions socially. Competing with other people provides a zest and a sharpness to action and winning the approval of others will perhaps elicit the greatest exertion. The careers of teaching, medicine, entertainment, administration and law will be the main occupations. Perhaps ninety-five percent of the public will move into them as permanent and freely chosen forms of activity. The honored occupations of physical construction and productivity will rapidly lose the satisfactions derived from public approval. This change can be best understood in looking at the most fundamental physical construction for man, the city, and its new degree of permanence.

ii. The New Monumentalism

American cities grew quickly. This was especially true of those in the latter half of the nineteenth century which followed the expansions of the railroads. Unlike the major cities of Western Europe which were slow in growing, and generally built with the best materials and best craftsmen of their time, the American buildings were spawned like prairie fires. Every man was his own designer and builder. Necessity due to scarcity, plus an idealism of democracy emphasized equality in professions and crafts of skilled with the unskilled. These two factors generated overnight cities that were inferior to the knowledge and materials of their times. The contrast between the physical structures of the European cities and those of America were often made by the magazines of the time.[1]

Cities like San Francisco, Chicago, and St. Louis were inundated with shabby dwellings of wood, hastily thrown up by unskilled builders. These buildings were highly susceptible to quick destruction. Fire, storms, and generally poor construction made short lives of many of these. Oklahoma City is proud of becoming a city of 20,000 in a few hours, but it could have been as easily disassembled in a few hours. The theme was to build and rebuild. The physical structures of America, with the exception of the eastern coastal cities which were largely built in the seventeenth and eighteenth centuries, contributed to a revolutionary and rapidly changing existence. Thus, America was in better position than Western Europe to dismantle and move to a mature urbanized civilization when it appeared on the horizon. The world wars and their destruction, especially the leveling of Germany, created a similar climate in Europe where the building durable to natural elements finally succumbed to an irrational bestiality of man himself. A great deal of human effort was constantly necessary to keep man in some kind of shelter; this was especially true for shoddy building. They may have required a short time and little skill to construct initially, but the maintenance and replacement of the structure in the long run required more.

America in the twentieth century is a different case, especially in the last few decades. It is now constructing a monumental physical structure parallel to that of a historic Rome or London. The best materials, the best information of the time, the best architects, the best craftsmen are now in the process of building and rebuilding the American physical environment and it is designed to last a thousand years. The excitement of this period of construction fills our magazines, newspapers, books, and all other means of communication. Each city concentration competes with others for durability and attractiveness, and builders and architects are held in the highest esteem. Like all monuments they strive to make them permanent, immortal, and barring extremely destructive wars the probability is that they will be here in the year 2000 and also in the year 2100. As some architects and artists fear, in their dislike for particular construction, these same buildings will remain to determine our lives for the rest of this generation and the next. With each structure there is less opportunity for architects and builders.

It is not difficult to identify these monuments since they include a great majority of the buildings recently completed or presently under way. They are the "new" Boston, the "new" Philadelphia, the "new" Chicago, the "new" St. Louis, the "new" Pittsburgh. There is hardly a city in America that is not reconstructing itself in this new monumentalism, in both private and public buildings. The sheer beauty and massiveness can hardly be described in words. Pictures or on-site visits give a much better impression of this aspiration to permanence.

The optimism is naturally high that this rebuilding will go on and on, at an even faster rate. Visionary architects are not satisfied with the Rockefeller Plaza of New York City or the Golden Triangle of Pittsburgh. Their designs run to entirely new "Platform cities, Motopias, Multi-tiered cities," and cities strung in long lines. There is no doubt that some of these will be built in part, and will suffer the success and failure of all other designs. But the crucial point to be made here is that the presently constructed monumentalisms will remain. They will be refurnished, remodeled, but their maintenance economy and their beauty will dictate a rationale to preserve. Our children and grandchildren will be housed and will work and re-create in the physical facilities already here. Innovation will not have the virgin space of the past; it will have to compete with an operational structure, with beauty, with history, with alternatives to spend the time consuming rather than producing.

It is not difficult to test this hypothesis. One needs only to go over the buildings that have been constructed since new materials have been available during the past seventy-five years, and the answer is apparent. The well-designed and well-built building is still with us in ninety percent of the cases. It is too valuable to tear down.

A great number of these new types of buildings never existed in history, i.e., the modern factories like those of the automobile industry, the skyscrapers made possible by the use of the new materials, the shopping centers made possible by the wide use of the automobile, and finally, the stadia for the leisured public.

The railroad system in America is another good illustration of our tendency to preserve the well-built and well-designed product. Most of the present railroads were built by the turn of the century, and they are still here in repaired fashion, hauling as much as they did then. Their decline is relative rather than absolute. The tremendous expansion of the population and the new mobility gave new forms of transportation, the automobile and the airplane, their business. But the reader must recall that one of the fundamental assumptions of this book is a decreasing expansion of population in the highly urbanized regions. This means that old methods and old facilities will have to be displaced rather than new ones providing new services for new customers.

One of the most weighty investments of this new monumentalism is the construction of the great new superhighways. Their cost will be too heavy to replace them in a short time, and like the old Roman roads which survived Rome by a thousand years, they are likely to persist that long. What of the growth of new means of transportation? The cost of displacement will have to be measured against staying with the existing operations, and the new will often play a losing game. Karl Marx feared that the limitation of change was a function of ownership. He was to be corrected by economic thought which more realistically measures change as the product of *all* the alternatives to the use of human energy. On this ground the odds are against displacement. Economy won't of course be the only basis for retention of the existing. Style could be as vital a factor in bringing about change. By style in building I don't mean fads or variations on the theme. True and fundamental style changes are as rare as basic economic revolutions. A truly new style of building has accompanied the urban-universal revolution and it is likely to be just as permanent as the social, economic and political changes accompanying the urban-universal revolution. We might therefore find it fruitful to examine briefly architectural style itself.

iii. *The Appearance of a New Universal Style of Architecture*

The agri-provincial civilization found its unity and its answers to the problems of life in the Church. Its great monuments were the pyramids, the temples, and the cathedrals. The unity of the urban-universal civilization is in its centers of learning, its public educational institutions, its colleges and universities. They are also rapidly becoming the indisputable sources for the answers to the problems of life man faces. They are generating and dictating the architectural style of our urban man-designed structures.

Modern architecture, perhaps more than any other medium, can most fully communicate the transition in human living. As the great Swiss historian of architecture Sigfried Giedion states, "It is the product of all sorts of factors—social, economic, scientific, technical, ethnological . . ."[2] It is the unity between the new and historical, between the artistic and the strictly functional. Thus, in examining this area it is not surprising to find the grand statements made about architecture.

One of the important architects of our time, Peter Blake, opens his book *The Master Builders* with the following:

> At no time in recorded history of architecture has the manner in which men build undergone change as radical as those that have occurred during the past century. Under the pressure of the tremendous growth in earth's population, new developments took place . . . nowhere more spectacular than in the field of architecture.
>
> Because more and more people had to be housed and employed in large centers, builders had to learn to build vertically. Technology provided two essential tools: the steel-framed building that could rise to great heights without requiring enormously thick walls at ground level; and the mechanical elevator.[3]

This is an attitude not uniformly held. A fine architect like Victor Gruen, in his book *The Heart of Our Cities*, devotes a chapter to the apparent chaotic state of architecture.[4] But such criticism seems more of impatience at not fully implementing a style than a criticism of the entire absence of one. Gruen recognizes the "master builders" as such. Perhaps Giedion answers the charge best when he says "that in spite of the seeming confusion there is nevertheless a true, if hidden unity, a secret synthesis, in our present civilization."[5]

Who are the acknowledged leaders, the "master builders" of this new school of architecture? When did it really begin? The answer to these questions is surprisingly uniform by all respected writers in the field. Modern architecture, or what sometimes is called the "International Style," had its birth unquestionably during the past century. It was preceded by a host of basic inventions and various technological innovations which made it possible and without which the modern school would be inconceivable. Steel, Portland cement, elevators, electricity, telephones, mass production, etc., were all products or techniques that have come into existence since 1850. During the following seventy-five years they were experimented with until an extensive use and knowledge of them could be intertwined in a single building by a single architect. Louis Sullivan in the United States of the 1890s is credited with almost single-handedly perfecting the skyscraper.[6] Frank Lloyd Wright harmoniously integrated the technologies with humanistic ideals at the turn of the century. But if there is one man in the world who can be identified as consciously founding a universal formula for modern architecture and uncompromisingly implanting it upon the world it has to be Walter Gropius of Germany.

Gropius, who was born in 1883 into the family of a Berlin architect, is neither the earliest of the new school nor has he been the most productive. To him goes the honor of making the first clear statement about all the facets of modern architecture. Sigfried Giedion dates the initiation of the new period of art and architecture, cognizant of its new dimensions of space and material, about 1910 with Picasso and Gropius.[7] The new form, new style, apparently reaches its clear mastery about 1926 or 1927. It is during this period that Gropius is credited with making a sharp break with past forms. A biographer of Gropius says that his first major work, the Fagus factory in 1911, was such a clear statement of the new form that it displayed an "absolute freedom from any dependence upon historic form."[8] Thus Gropius is not considered a transitional figure but one whose work lies wholly on the side of the modern movement. He did not rely upon ornamentation. His buildings separated skeleton and skin, having the weight on the frame and the walls hanging rather than being supportive. He used new materials of glass, concrete and steel in ways that are now commonplace.[9]

The Fagus creation became consciously formalized by Gropius into a school of philosophy regarding architecture. His founding of the Bauhaus in April 1919 brought together in a single school under a single roof the ingredients of the new style. It has gone under titles of Bauhaus, Functional, International or Modern. The Bauhaus movement became the educational leader for the others to follow or to measure themselves against.

The philosophy of the Bauhaus was to emphasize the interdependence of creative work regarding all aspects of the building, foundation, furniture, curtains, outside landscaping, etc. In a world rapidly moving towards specialization, which he recognized, Gropius emphasized the need for collaboration rather than individual and separate activity. He never wavered in this approach even after fifteen years as the head of the School of Architecture at Harvard University between 1937 and 1952. This was at the time when the king of all American architects, Frank Lloyd Wright, was championing the complete freedom for the individual architect. Thus, while Wright's creations may remain more outstanding, his philosophy is a romantic throwback to an earlier period.

A social historian of American architecture, Wayne Andrews, separates the Gropiuses from the Wrights by calling the first category the Veblenites after Thorstein Veblen, who emphasized efficiency and economy.[10] The Wrights he labels Jacobites who yearned to be more personal and individualistic. The impact on the world by the Veblenites is immediately obvious by the names Andrews lists in this category, and for whom he expresses less sympathy. After Gropius there is Mies van der Robe, Le Corbusier, Oud, Eero Saarinen, Kahn, and others who might be considered the "great masters" or quantity producers. On the Jacobite side after Wright would be a few influential architects known internationally.

The development of this new style of architecture, free from the traditions of thousands of years, is not in question. Frank Lloyd Wright, Walter Gropius, or present leaders like I. M. Pei are all using the new materials, building functionally and artistically in terms of the urban civilization. There is rapidly emerging an appreciation of the beauty of their work and a desire to preserve it and repeat it in some variation. There is a growing attitude to preserve their work as the monuments of the past have been preserved. The monuments today are created not only for the kings as was the case in the past, but for the entire public. Just as the kings of the past had an attitude for permanence in their castles, the urban public is now developing this same attitude toward permanence of their shopping centers, apartment buildings, office buildings, in fact, their entire land and seascapes.

iv. *Planning—A Formula Applicable to Change and Stability (Paradox)*

Intrinsically tied with the new architectural style is a technical formula that has been an incentive to rapid change, "planning." While this formula is not new in human history it, nevertheless, has been absent during the major portion of the urban-universal revolution. Its recurrence recently as a beneficial formula to production is a paradox. It appears to have that quality of encouraging change initially, but in the long run its consequences lead to greater stability than change.

The key to understanding what is happening in this respect is to focus on this revolutionary concept in urban society. We hear of the planned economy, the planned society, planned parenthood, planned conservation of resources, etc. These are ideas that dominate communist, socialist and capitalist systems equally. This has been especially true since 1945, the end of World War II. There is resistance to it in most countries, especially to national and international planning but the tendency is to think increasingly in terms of longer-range plans—five-, ten-, and even fifty-year plans.

One reason for some continued resistance to national planning is its opposition to certain private plans. Another and perhaps more basic opposition is that planning has been associated with revolutionary change. Soviet society popularized planning on a national scale while they were experiencing their greatest social and economic change. It has thus been as difficult to extricate this aspect of human behavior from the Soviet connotation as to separate the word democracy from association with the United States. The rest of the world had a hard time adopting a universal process first popularized in the United States as something of its own, and now the same is true for the USSR. The fact that both were the most trumpeted systems of a general trend appears obscured especially by these two nations. Thus, if we are to appreciate the role of planning in urbanized society we must see it as a universal development and understand it for what it is rather than the specific form in which we may have seen it.

Planning means disciplining ourselves for longer range

goals when an immediate rationale or immediate tempta-
tion would demand a closer satisfaction. For a people that
have become accustomed to living for today because tomorrow is so uncertain it becomes a painful readjustment.
Building roads for the future, conserving resources for a
hundred years hence, lending money on a forty-year basis,
constructing twenty-five-year master plans for cities did
not appear rational when the next day's invention may
completely change the form that is being planned. The
reason it is becoming rational, and widely accepted today
is that we can increasingly count on conditions ten, twenty
or thirty years hence as being not unlike the present.

The important thing about planning in regard to its
capacity for permitting change is its long range goals. Are
they the goals of the Soviets for a transition from rural
to urban society? If so, then they will augur a dizzy pace of
change. Are they the goals of the British which prepare
themselves to retain maximum security for the individual
and maximum opportunity for leisurely existence? If so,
the physical structure remains stable. The United States
is equally bent on freeing the individual from work to
play, from a life of producing potatoes to a life of golf;
from a life of producing steel to a life of camping in national parks; from a life of toil to one of entertainment.
The planning, therefore, that the most advanced urban
societies are increasingly experiencing is a reduction of
production. The seventy-two-hour week to the forty-hour
week to the twenty-four-hour week, and on to the guaranteed annual wage for the nonworker. Nonworking is a
contagious stage, and once attained will not easily be surrendered. If increased productivity is not in demand for
nonworking it will not come. Nonworking consumption
does not have to be high. Most of the greatest pleasures

do not require great production. A day in the country, on the seashore, or international travel can now be done with small cost of the productive structure. Once the physical plant is built so that it takes no more to keep it than to replace it, and once some of the simple necessities of life, food, shelter, clothing and transportation are produced with the minimum of human work, it is going to be tremendously difficult to get those who have a great deal of leisure time to give it up. Thus, planning can be equally for an equilibrium as for dynamic change. And the planning in the Western democracies will prefer the leisurely life to one of production for production's sake. The avant garde of today, in America and Britain especially, are not anxious to participate in competitive production as a game, not when they can compete more economically as human personalities.

Notes: Chapter 5

1. Victor Gruen, *The Heart of Our Cities,* New York, Simon & Schuster, 1964, pp. 30–31.
2. Sigfried Giedion, *Space, Time and Architecture* (The growth of a new tradition), Cambridge, Mass., Harvard University Press, 1946, p. 19.
3. Peter Blake, *The Master Builders,* New York, Alfred A. Knopf, 1961, preface.
4. Gruen, *op. cit.,* Chapter 12.
5. Giedion, *op. cit.,* p. v.
6. Wayne Andrews, *Architecture, Ambition, and Americans,* Glencoe, Ill., The Free Press, 1964.
7. Giedion, *op. cit.,* p. 401.
8. James M. Fitch, *Walter Gropius,* New York, George Braziller, 1960, p. 20.
9. *Ibid.,* p. 19.
10. Andrews, *op. cit.,* Chapter 7.

6. THE INTELLECTUAL GENESIS OF THE NEW ORDER

i. *The Revolution Shatters Old Values of Individualism and Freedom*

When the last vestiges of military authority are gone in a defeated army, the individual must accept the responsibility of looking out for himself. In the Hobbesian sense, the commitment of the individual to the political organization is binding only as long as the organization can provide security for him. If the authorities can no longer guarantee some order they cannot expect obedience. While the above analogy cannot be transferred exactly to the point under consideration it nevertheless gives a good comparison of what was true of a comparable situation in the early nineteenth century in Western Europe. The agricultural-provincial society of that period was being pressed back like an army in the field, into smaller and smaller areas of control, leaving great numbers of stragglers and deserters to the victorious armies of industry and urbanization. These alienated rural troops were "used" by the victors wherever they could fit in, and if there was no use for them they were literally sacrificed, to hunger, slow starvation, disease, overwork, despondency, and the mercy or brutality of the police. This was the period of rapid transition between new foundations of life; this was the revolution at its peak periods.

101

It is little wonder that the nineteenth century is sometimes referred to as the "ugliest century" in history, even
though it was also one of great innovation and creativity.
Nor is there any wonder that between 1815 and 1914 there
were no large-scale international conflicts. As a substitute
there was a constant internal war, a civil war going on
between the new civilization and the old in the most advanced industrial countries of the world. This served all
the functions that conflict might possibly serve in human
organization, without any need of inventing new conflicts.

The nineteenth-century Western European industrial
civilization produced great numbers of alienated people,
cut off from their previous moorings and unable to find
a new home and new roots in the city. Here was anomic
man so extensively described by the social scientists. Here
was the lonely individual, "mass man," unable to exercise
his old rural skills and believe in his old provincial values
because they no longer applied in his new situation. The
new conditions had no ready-made "place" for him to fit
into. He was told that he was better off because he was
now free, and that freedom was more important than anything else in the world. He accepted it in Russia as freed
from serfdom, in America as freed from slavery, and
throughout the urbanized world as freed from the land
and the vicious landlords. He accepted this freedom because he had no alternative, but he did not relish it, and
as Erich Fromm so ably demonstrated, he tried to "escape
from this freedom."[1]

What kind of freedom was it? The freed peasant, serf
or slave, was now free to go anywhere but he had no
money for transportation. He was free to seek any job,
but all but the unskilled jobs were closed to him, and
even these at times were scarce. He was free from family

or religious control but who wanted this freedom. Thus it never was difficult for the Marxists, the political dictators to win large followings from these "free men" by promising to actually take away their freedom and substitute it with a meal, a job, a cause, a place in the world if they would surrender their freedoms. Since freedom is meaningless unless you have real alternatives, it was no surprise that "uprooted farmers chose the authority that promised to deliver these wants over the end of unlimited but also an unrealized freedom."

The avant-garde intellectuals who had seen the obsolete character of the agri-provincial society and lambasted it from all sides by claiming that it had an unwholesome hold over the individual argued for freedom. But when they were forced to face the problem of what a man was to do with this freedom they recoiled in horror that someone should even ask. They were in a dilemma. They could not honestly argue for another enslavement by a new industrial organization, especially when the new order was itself so nebulous and less attractive than the old. Yet, with the exception of Rousseau, neither could they see the individual become civilized without society. And Rousseau was of course totally wrong about society.

ii. *The Iconoclasts of the Old Order*

Jeremy Bentham and John Stuart Mill are good examples of the iconoclasts of the old order and reluctant heretics of the new. Bentham never even tried to face the question of what the individual was to do with his freedom from provincial authority. It was enough for him, as it had earlier been for Montesquieu in France, to show how ridiculous were the agri-provincial authorities in an urban-universal world. J. S. Mill, who was either more honest or more perceptive, saw the obligation of answering the question of how even a single individual could fruitfully and with dignity employ his freedom. He realized that it was impossible without a formal education, and this was a social matter, a product of order and authority, which to exist required certain limitations on everyone's freedom. By the end of Mill's life he had rationalized giving up many of the individuals' freedoms in order to reap the benefits of industry, education, the arts, and most of all a responsibility by society for the individual. Mill accepted this, but could not champion it.[2]

Marx, a contemporary of Mill, was as effective an iconoclast as the earlier Bentham; but unlike Mill, Marx found no conflict in preaching the advantages of the new order over the old. While Marx saw the new foundation of life based upon large agglomerations of people and property of a scale too large or too important for individual ownership, he still failed to face the human problems of how an urbanized individual was to use his freedom, politically, morally, socially, and privately.[3] John Stuart Mill was ahead of his time and of Marx in dealing with society in terms of its obligations to the individual in fostering and preserving real alternatives. In this respect he was also ahead of his liberal socialist followers in Britain and America who sold out to majority rule as the sole determiner of human welfare. Neither majority rule nor the promise of truth triumphing in the open market place was sufficient for him. For Mill there had to be a real alternative to the prevailing philosophy even if artificially created and supported. He saw that the individual could be stifled as easily by the majoritarian ethic as it had often been earlier by tradition or class.

Of the nineteenth-century political philosophers, Edmund Burke today might seem the most modern and most advanced in his thinking and should increasingly become a twentieth-century hero. This is, however, a misrepresentation of his place in comparison to the preceding thinkers. For while he is apropos of our times in advocating a philosophy of stability, tradition and slow change, he made the mistake of misreading his own century or revolution. The Frenchman Alexis de Tocqueville was probably the most profound political observer in terms of understanding his own times and the potential future. While he saw the wave of "equalitarianism" as the dynamo of the revolution all over the world, he also looked to a way and a time when quality and human greatness would maintain itself in the world. His *Democracy In America* is as apropos of political and social life in the 1960s as it was in the 1830s, and as it will be a century from now. It fails in achieving the stature of a Plato's *Republic* only because he failed to generalize his assessment sufficiently.

The nineteenth-century writers of fiction fared no better, if as well, in extricating themselves from their own milieu, and put man in a greater historical perspective. Change, revolution, progress, evolution, and empirical optimism were the order of the day and they made their heroes and their projections in this respect. While George Bernard Shaw and Thomas Carlyle would not accept fully the "egalitarian" ethic, they went along with John Henry Newman, Thomas Babington Macaulay, Tennyson and Kipling in England, and with Whitman in America in eulogizing progress and change. It was a literature of rebellion and adventure. The struggle of the individual in the nineteenth century was to pit him against natural odds like the pioneer against the forces of nature, the industrial worker against the external odds in the form of other people, the boss, the labor union leader, the corrupt organization. Another favorite theme was the *nouveau riche* against the aristocracy, or against their selfish less successful. These authors saw the adventure of mankind in a contest with external forces.

How different have been the literary creations of the post-World War I era in the twentieth century. They too portray their own milieu and it is in a different period. Writers like Franz Kafka, William Faulkner, T. S. Eliot, James Joyce almost uniformly turn inward and look at man's soul. The struggle is internal and not external. The answers of these writers, if answers there are, is not to flee to new adventure, but to retreat, pacifism, renewal, and accommodation. If the literature of the two groups described tends to reflect their times the difference between the two centuries is drawn sharply. And if Karl Marx was the leading exponent of social direction in the nineteenth century looking outwardly to change and revolution, then Sigmund Freud is the equivalent in the mid-twentieth century, looking inward to peace and stability. There can be no victory in the internal struggle, since the enemy is always a part of the self. There can only be a compromise, a reconciliation.[4]

iii. *The Reluctant Perception of the New Order*

The challenge now is of course to spell out how the individual is to find his place, his identity in a world that is again settling down to a new set of authorities and order. The books for our times which identify this problem talk about an urban society that is rapidly becoming stratified, bureaucratized, and not subject to rapid change. Their fears of man becoming enslaved are exaggerated, as artists always must, but their consensus on the new problem is unmistakable. The previously anomic man is now becoming the conformist organization man. In psychology he is exemplified by such works as Riesman's *The Lonely Crowd,* Fromm's *Man for Himself,* or Whyte's *Organization Man.* In sociology and political science the individual is viewed as being controlled by a hierarchical elite, i.e. Mills' *The Power Elite,* and a great number of works which do not dispute hierarchy, but only ask whether it is fluid or rigid. Sociology also exemplifies it in the extensive devotion to the study of class led by the Lynds and Warner. The economists who have taken the lead have only a few exceptions from the stable economy and the equilibrium thesis. The most significant work in this area has been Galbraith's *The Affluent Society.*

These new traditional authorities are different and much harder to identify, in part because they have only begun to crystallize. The authority that was internalized in the past was the heritage of centuries, and could always be located in a given place. If some palace revolution or war displaced them a new authority, essentially the same in nature took their place. The new traditional authorities emerging in our urban society are not limited to a location because it would be impossible for them to survive in a society that is so highly mobile. To survive today they have to be as flexible and mobile as the people they would control. Thus the modern organized authority, even though chartered in a given place, having located a headquarters in a given place is not limited to place. It is this new authority of organizational life that lies at the base of stability in our society. They are putting boundaries on change. These gigantic political, economic and social organizations are the new cement that is binding mobile urban man into a community. They are not transitory organizations. Many now have survived a century or more of existence. And as Whyte so frantically describes them in *Organization Man,* they restrict freedom and innovation in their demands for order and unity.

The industrial organization, the professional organization, the fraternal organization have become national, and more recently international. A few years ago Charles Ferguson more aptly described them in his book *Fifty Million Brothers:*

> . . . They have grown and multiplied simply because they provided the only natural basis for normal group life in a country historically deprived of it. To achieve a semblance of unity it has been necessary to band together in associations, clubs, grottoes, lodges, temples, nests, droves, hives, shrines, shelters, commanderies, encampments, wigwams, leagues, herds, mystic circles, and other sanctums.[5]

These organizations follow the city dweller, and are already at the new location to meet him when he moves. An "organizational revolution" has taken place, says Kenneth Boulding, as does William Whyte, but what they don't emphasize is the new nature of this organizational revolution. Civilized man has always had organization and hierarchical authority. But the urban-universal organization has conquered space. A stranger in the United States today who changes an occupation by moving a thousand miles finds that he is still a member of a number of corporate bodies. There are records that are available to anyone for a small fee that reveal him to scrutiny as careful as any ever administered in the small town or village which controlled him in the past. The system through these records, described earlier in the book, extends greater and greater control over any variation from the norm. This is the condition that Whyte bemoans:

> Blood brother to the business trainee off to join Du Pont is the seminary student who will end up in the church hierarchy, the doctor headed for the corporate clinic, the physics Ph.D. in a government laboratory, the intellectual on the foundation sponsored team project, the engineering graduate in the huge drafting room at Lockheed, the young apprentice in a Wall Street law factory.[6]

There is no question in Whyte's mind that the individual has fallen prey to the organizational social ethic in America, nor is there any expectation from him that man could end the control of the social ethic.[7] His only hope is for man, as an individual, to retain a dignity and an identity that is not identical with the organization. This suspicion of the overwhelming organizational demands may be greater in the United States than in other countries.[8] But no industrial nation has emerged without a complex organizational structure.

Thus the psychological pulls stemming from needs of security and identity are being defined by the new national and international organizations which have emerged in the past hundred years replacing the controls of the agri-provincial authorities which have gradually eroded into obscurity. These new economic, professional, and fraternal organizations are not fleeting structures. They will be here fifty years hence and they will have established ways of accommodation between themselves and will be defining the roles of the individual within them. Man will be born into stabilized organizational structures. This is already apparent in our discovery of a greater willingness of the younger generation to seek the security of big organizations and submission to their demands rather than choosing the less secure. While the older generation may think adventure is of greater value than stability there is no more proof than those who prefer stability. Nor can we prove that aggression is better than pacifism and accommodation, nor that uncompromising principles are better than compromise. The organization man is not suited for a revolutionary society, but a more fundamental question may be: Can the adventurous revolutionary man find satisfaction in a stable social-economic system?

The present generation may occasionally display symptoms of the Luddites, and relish the revolt against the machine. But we tend to leave these wishes only to the realm of fiction like *Utopia 14*, or to the vicarious pleasures of the uncompromising savage in *Brave New World*. In practice even the older, more recalcitrant generation likes the fruits of organizational life, and here is the pull to stability for both the older and younger generation in the urbanized world.

Two books which have received a great deal of serious and popular attention in England and America which are supposedly predictive of the coming of the end of progress and revolutionary change are Aldous Huxley's *Brave New World*, originally published in 1932, and George Orwell's *1984*, originally published in 1949. In the years following World War II, when our imaginations had already been stirred by the atomic bomb and by the Cold War, these two books became companion landmarks of description of the destiny of the most advanced nations of the world. While Utopias painted by neither of these two books was fully acceptable, there seemed little question that they were rapidly approaching reality. The interesting thing about both these books was that they painted a fixed, controlled, stable world.

While there can be no definite proof of why these two books remained the fundamental academic bill-of-fare for the two decades following World War II, the suspicion is strong that they satisfied a need, a desire for stability. While both were real enough they were also unattractive enough to resist any immediate fixed order. The urban-universal revolution was near then but had not reached its peak anywhere in the world. The changes necessary following World War II, especially in the highly urbanized countries demanded the maintainment of a high degree of anxiety, at least until the economies devastated by the war were reconstructed.

iv. *Inching Towards Stability in Western Europe and the United States*

To want something is not necessarily to have it, but to have the desire for something and some opportunity of realizing it will be highly indicative of the actions a person or a group will take in such a situation. This was the situation of a war-weary public in 1945 in the highly industrialized countries of the world. Their choice was for security, stability, peace and the enjoyment of the fruits of industrial production. It was not for more change and adventure, despite the fact that both were still in store for these nations, and especially for America.

The English, the French, German and American have given full indication that their desire has been for security and stability. This has also been true of the Soviets but in 1945 it was physically impossible for them to realize it at that stage.

Western Germany is an excellent example of the yearning for security in preference to revolution. During the years 1949–1964 in which they had relative control over their economy and their government, they chose to rebuild quickly what was destroyed. They tended to do it in terms of their previously urbanized economy, with products based on quality and durability rather than innovation. The Volkswagen automobile was the most significant symbol of this direction. It was modest, durable, designed for performance and not for experimentation and rapid obsolescence. The West Germans were very reluctant to invest heavily in innovation for their industrial rebuilding. They were also reluctant to participate in a new rearmament. They were reluctant to follow adventuresome policies regardless of their great desire for a national reunification for Germany. And when they had a chance to express themselves politically, they chose the promised stability of Konrad Adenauer rather than the parties for great change.

The British choice in 1945 appeared to be a nation bent on social and economic revolution. The election of the Labour Party with their program of nationalization appeared to be a Marxian promise come true that the British people, if any, might be able to bring about a revolution without violence. It is now apparent that the British revolution, in so far as it was a revolution, was the choice for greater security and stability and not for a program of accelerated innovation. Economic security was uppermost, and cutting off the mother country from a great part of the Empire was not a move for adventure, but for retreat. The social security which was to increase the individual's freedom to mobility, socially and economically, was to reduce anxiety and not to encourage innovation. It was to satisfy an existing situation of a mobile population that needed a guarantee against the unemployment and social anonymity suffered by the great bulk of the British population between the two great wars.

These reforms in Britain were a realistic acceptance of a performance at a modest but stable level. The preceding organization was geared for higher performance but was actually realizing less. Finally when there were some signs that the political structure was truly going to experiment economically and socially it was replaced by those who promised no new experiments. England is supposedly now, as are the Scandinavian countries, suffering from a boredom with the security and stability, manifesting it in higher suicide rates among the older citizens, and destructive rebellion by the younger. This may well be the price a social system has to pay for stability. But these acts appear little more than the exception which proves the rule. They make us conscious of the rule and of human independence.

France as a highly industrial nation has been an equally good example of a nation choosing stability over new adventure. The separation of itself from Indo-China and Algeria were extreme measures undertaken to bring about stability in preference to adventure. DeGaulle's victory was added indication of a return to traditional authority in a country that was completing the urban-universal revolution.

The case of the United States as a nation choosing security and stability since the war is less clear. In the twenty years following World War II the American foreign and domestic actions indicate a nation in revolution. From a country of isolationism politically we became the experimenters in the use of the U.N., limited war, and various social and economic programs to bring about a change in international conditions in Europe and the less developed parts of the world.

It was apparent that initially international stability was the American choice. Immediately following World War II the United States made a rapid retreat from international responsibility with the expectation that stability would be a natural consequence. The U.N. had been created to deal with the irrepressible conflicts that might grow out of unsettled conditions, while we expected to commit our time and resources to our own satisfactions of our highly industrialized economy. Western Europe, and the Soviet Union especially, were faced with the great problem of postwar reconstruction and refused to give the United States the choice of international withdrawal.

The Western European nations demanded that the United States continue to play an important world policing role. They also expected the continuation of United States support to be transferred from the previous military to industrial rebuilding. The United States had been in the same war as they, but whereas their nations bore the brunt of the battle, being heavily devastated, the United States actually benefited in developing and expanding its industrial capability. The Soviets were of the same opinion, but ideologically found it difficult to seek assistance in a way that would be demanded by a country diametrically opposed to their ideology.

The Western European nations were thus able to reverse America's initial preference for international withdrawal by threatening to unify with the Communist world for their reconstruction if the United States persisted in its withdrawal. The potential enemy that such a successful union might create militarily and for world markets shocked both the United States political and economic communities to a very substantial reversal of the withdrawal policy. The Cold War with our Truman Doctrine, Marshall Plan, NATO, etc., became one of the prices we paid for delaying the full fruits of our industrial capability.·

Nor could the United States fully experience its desire for stability in dealing with matters of a purely domestic nature. The United States was the first nation on the scene of affluence. The systematic application of science to industry, the bountiful resources of a country that suffered no internal destruction from war since 1865, resulted in a condition of glut, of surplus, of potentially disturbing unemployment, of serious union-management difficulties, of great disequilibrium. Grotesque monstrosities of instability were being suffered for which the world had no precedent. Unions resorted to extensive featherbedding, the preservation of a job after it became obsolete. It is small wonder that the nation also experienced widely a psychology of "something for nothing" which was morally and intellectually depressing for the nation.

Advertising also contributed to the promotion of a misjudgment of purpose, values, and a misallocation of resources that caused further confusion in the nation. Advertising was assigned the responsibility of influencing the people to use up all the produced resources whether they were good or not. Books like *The Affluent Society* and more popular ones like the *Wastemakers* tried to bring perspective. Others dealing with automation and cybernation tried to point out what was happening to the traditional areas of work and the need for us to find new ways of using our time and new ways of organizing ourselves. Labor, management and government organizations came forth with a multitude of solutions to deal with these matters, from a lowering of work hours to subsidies to industries which would bring a more balanced schedule of production. The immediate solution the American public chose was "a baby boom," the production of more "consumers," more mouths to feed. While the "baby boom," coupled with our foreign aid program, worked temporarily, the solution they had always made in agricultural society where the surplus might be a temporary threat, was inapplicable in the urban-universal civilization.

Our desire to utilize the fruits of the end of the urban-universal revolution was therefore unsuccessful by either our foreign or domestic approach. We were like the Keynesian car, without a driver, redoubling our efforts without identifying our position or our goal. Fortunately the science of stability and equilibrium was rapidly developed, both in England and the United States. Goals were being defined. The American people accepted this science of economy in the late 1950s, and while faces at the political level changed, their programs were now being worked out by the new scientists of order, especially economists. By the 1960s change for the sake of change which was psychologically necessary for the continuation of the revolution had been effectively challenged by the rationality. Change and innovation had to address themselves to the question of whether it was economical, or whether it had quality. It was no longer necessary for the old, the traditional to defend its existence, but rather the new for coming into practice.

It is significant that W. W. Rostow's very provocative book on stages of economic growth entitles the present stage of the highly industrial nations as the stage of economic "maturity." This term when applied to plants or animals means that they have reached their full growth.

In the biological sense it means that emotionally and physically the mature human being is not going to go through the drastic and sharp change that occurred from infancy through adulthood. Thus if the term means the same economically, our economy of high mass consumption has only one rational alternative, to relax and begin enjoying the satisfaction of maturity. It is inconceivable that war and destruction would be the rational choice, although it might happen accidentally. It is more inconceivable that the urban-universal civilization will be replaced even by the exploration of outer space since with stability our investments there will dwindle to the contributions the agricultural civilization made to the investments of the Arctic and Antarctic after they were discovered. They will generate the imagination more than they will investment.

Psychologically we were not ready in 1945 or in the 1950s to transfer our agri-provincial beliefs fully to urban-universal. We were still frightened and uncertain of our new condition and retreated to solutions we had known before. This, however, was a temporary aberration which is being reversed in the 1960s. We are psychologically better prepared today to accept the security, prosperity and leisure that we have worked for so long. It will be difficult for adventurers, innovators, and revolutionists to counter this orientation since it squares with our physical reality.

Notes: Chapter 6

1. Erich Fromm, *Escape from Freedom,* New York, Holt, 1941. It is the theme of the book.
2. Compare J. S. Mill's almost poetic essay *On Liberty* written in 1859, strongly defending freedom of the individual, to his *Auto-*

biography published in 1873 where he argues unenthusiastically for a social responsibility.

3. While Marx identified the illnesses of Capitalism in the hardships it created for the workingman at a given period in history, his writings never went far enough to describe how his utopia would deal with the problems of urbanism and socialism on a large scale. Marx also failed to see the successful combinations of private ownership and management on a widely disseminated basis like American Telephone and Telegraph or General Electric with only a modicum of public regulation. Nor did it ever occur to Marx that one of the major freedoms the urbanized man would seek would be privacy and not greater socialization.

4. Sigmund Freud, in his *Civilization and Its Discontents,* concludes that man's biological demands place a severe limitation on his ability to modify himself.

5. Charles Ferguson, *Fifty Million Brothers,* New York, Farrar and Rinehart, 1937. pp. 14–15.

6. William Whyte, *Organization Man,* p. 3.

7. A comprehensive development of the subject regarding the extent to which the social ethic has become a vital part of the 20th century urban living can be found in Hannah Arendt's *The Human Condition.*

8. Since traditional authority in Western Europe was never shed as completely as in America their transition to a new controlling authority of the organization is treated with less fear and apprehension though certainly not with any less question of its demands.

7. THE DECLINE OF POLITICAL AUTHORITY AS AN INDICATION OF STABILITY

i. *The Apparent Condition of Increasing Political Authority*

One of the most common manifestations of the urbanized civilizations is their rather uniform tendency to place more and more of their activity under political authority. Studying the expansion of government during the past fifty years, and especially the past thirty, one gets the impression that in the near future every urban activity will be directed and regulated by a centrally located political authority. Max Weber, the great German social scientist, was among the first to call our attention to this phenomenon and also was the first to provide the language by which we could examine it. He pursued the political authority through its many Protean manifestations and bearded the god in its den. According to Weber:

> There is scarcely any task that some political association has not taken in hand, and there is no task that one could say has always been exclusive and peculiar to these associations which are designated as political ones.[1]

Political authority has been so active during the past few years that we not only disagree on what it looks like but agree that whatever it is, it is all devouring and gaining increasing control over our minds, bodies, and other properties of mankind. One of the unquestioned assumptions being made today is the unrestrained growth of this multi-faced authority. Whether the question is raised in nations like the United States, where government has long been viewed with suspicion, or in the Soviet Union where it is viewed as the "new savior," it is equally recognized as gaining in a variety of forms and quantity. Political leaders like Lenin, Stalin, Hitler, and Mussolini are supposed to have risen to power on this wave. Franklin D. Roosevelt, Lyndon Johnson, and de Gaulle indicate that the democracies are not immune to this apparent tendency, nor that there is any decrease in political forms or quantity.

Empirical proof hardly seems necessary to demonstrate this condition in the United States; however, an indication of the degree of this escalation might be in order. One of the standard texts on American government dramatizes this multi-faced growth of government by titling the first chapter "The New Leviathan."[2] Viewing the various operations of government, every facet appears on the increase with new forms emerging rapidly while old ones disappear more slowly. Perhaps the most significant statistic listed is that between 1861 to 1961, while the number of federal employees increased eighty times, the United States population increased only six times.[3] And while the Eisenhower years may feebly have attempted to call a halt to extension of federal authority, President Johnson again was treated as desiring to advance political authority at a faster rate than any President before him. While the Nixon administration is still new there are, as yet, no clear departures from this trend.

The above appears to be clear indication of the advance of political authority. All indications also appear to support its further extension in the United States and elsewhere. In socialist countries where the government has taken over the major industries, the extension of political authority might therefore be considered to have reached a stage of permanency and totality. The most complete stage might at present be identified as that of the Soviet Union, where the unquestioned supremacy of political authority would be extant in every segment of human endeavor. The study of government there is inevitably the study of every activity since all action must be subject to public and rational explanation, plus supported by administrative sanction.[4] These characteristics—publicity, rationality, and sanction—are probably the most concrete attributes of political authority, i.e., if we are to follow through with Weber's description of rational-legal authority as substantively representing all political authority.[5]

This apparent condition of increasing form and quantity of political anatomy, therefore, legitimately confronts man with a further question. Will political authority continue to grow, and at an increasing rate until all authority is political, or will it peak, stabilize, and actually begin to decline in regard to the other sources which command human action? This is undoubtedly one of the most crucial questions of our times. Is man to face George Orwell's total political spying society in *1984* or would it be any better in a benevolent form of a machine despot of *Utopia 14?*

The consequences of the extension of the above rate of political authority is without question the elimination of all other conflicting authorities. The *Leviathan* that Thomas Hobbes predicted would then be a reality beyond his dreams. The empirical evidence would be strong that before this century is out, the *Leviathan* would be realized, if the present trend is projected. Many graduate degrees in government could be earned by statistically projecting the rate toward politicization from country to country.

The point of this chapter, nevertheless, is to challenge the thesis of the coming *Leviathan*. The method is not by questioning the facts regarding the rate of growth of political authority as now defined, but actually by examining the nature of political authority itself and redefining it. For if all historical forms in which government has acted are to be admitted, especially those that become traditional, automatic reactions, plus all forms of public consent, then government may truly be considered completely pervasive. But at the same time the scientific aspects of the purpose of study, specialization, and prediction have been lost.

ii. *Completing the Scale of Measurement*

Government must be viewed as a process and not as a thing, and political authority must necessarily be viewed as increasing and diminishing under different circumstances. The greater the social segment subject to revision by force of legitimate group leadership, the greater is the political authority; conversely, the less of the social fabric available for such modification, the smaller the sphere of political authority. Man must be able to break from the utopian schools of progress to which Max Weber's categories inevitably lead, especially his categorization of authority into traditional and legal.[6] There is no doubt that a very valuable distinction for the study of government was made by Weber, but in using it he falls into the same trap as Marx did with Hegel, which was to make a certain stage in the cyclic theory a finished and permanent end. Thus, Max Weber's legal-rational category tends to be idealized and a pejorative connotation given to the traditional category, which makes it timebound and useless for analytical evaluation. Two current students of the subject commit the same error: Daniel Lerner in *The Passing of Traditional Society,* and David Riesman in *The Lonely Crowd.* Both treat the concept of traditional authority as a stage of the past rather than as a live alternative to the legal-rational continuum which must be done if the formula is to be a useful tool for measurement. Other current writers also appear unable to treat the concept of traditional authority without thinking about primitive, agriculturally based society. An exception to this group, at least in entertaining the feasibility of a more general and modern treatment of tradition, is Everett Hagen, who states the following:

> It is true that up to the present time there have been no traditional industrial societies. This, however, may be merely because the burst of innovation that brought industrialization has not had time to run its course. A train of events that will bring a return to traditionalism may even now be pursuing its inevitable sequence. . . .[7]

Thus if traditional authority is to be a meaningful category to contrast the legal-rational, political authority defined here, it must be divested of a once-and-for-all existence ascribed to it. While Weber is still the starting point, new life needs to be given to his contrasting categories of authority.

Weber's rational-legal authority was an attempt to

identify a force that in a time of great physical and social upheaval was attempting to accommodate, to adjust, to prevent friction between the old and the new. This force could, like Proteus, the prophetic old man of the sea in Greek mythology who could change himself into any form he pleased, come in varying forms—a bureau, a department, a prime minister, a president, a parliament, a law, etc. It broke through the previously held bonds of personal loyalty and myth by demanding an impersonal, rational, publicly recorded norm. It became heavily involved in social change. The generally accepted reason for this was that in many places it was the only force willing to assume the responsibility of transportation or any other function in a state of near chaos.[8]

The rational-legal authority of Weber became a clearly identifiable force, closely related to the developing science and technology. It was objective. Its rules had to be written and subject to a single interpretation by those not a part of the contracting arrangement. Like science and technology the roles of this force had to be spelled out, broken down into specialized function. Rewards and punishments had to be specifically prescribed and dominance and subordination were established as administrative and not personal relations. "Weber conceived of the world as becoming progressively rational and demystified, with corresponding change in organizational forms."[9] Here is where Weber did damage to his concept as a permanent measuring device.

While some injustices may appear, nevertheless, Weber's rational-legal authority can be equated with the legitimation and rationalization of force to obtain order.

At the base of this rationalization must always be "naked power," the power to command someone to do something because the powerful one has the force to make him obey. David Easton in his book on political theory said that political authority was the power to allocate values.[10] This indeed is the highest form of power one individual can have over another because it not only is a control over a person's physical actions but also over his mind. Yet it must be remembered that at the base, too, is force. Once force is removed or lost, the relationship between the commander and the recipient is no longer that of political authority regardless of how extensive is the willingness of one person to follow another, to emulate another or to be of service to another. If it is a relationship based on habit, love, identity, or aspiration, but not based on fear of bodily destruction, then we are in another realm of power. Thus, Weber's rational-legal authority is only meaningful when it is built on force. It has no meaningful political authority if it is built on one of the drives or forces of man where obedience is voluntary. It would be utterly naïve to assume that the word "rational" is a meaningful determinant without a means like the force to destroy, the force to love or preserve. Therefore, if political authority is to be separated from other authorities it must be limited to force. Politics, the mechanism which brings accommodation and is today a favorite activity for political scientists to study in America, is not a study of political authority. Herein lies a good deal of the misunderstanding of what is happening historically. A concentration on authority which has the power to destroy and whose immediate legitimacy is based on it will curtail two confusing areas now linked. First, the segment of authority that moved from traditional to political can be separated and carried the next step of the cycle which again moves back to traditional. Only then will it be a genuine measurement. Second, by separating a consensus politics from the force politics symbolized in political authority one can better predict the direction of social organization and behavior.

It is at the point of separating authority based on force from that based on love, economic performance, etc., that the subject becomes most controversial and confusing. Both friends and enemies of political authority contribute to the confusion by claiming too much. All ordering of society should not be treated as political. While politics is Protean, public, rational, dynamic, it is not the authority that relies upon love as does the family, or monetary gain as does the economy, or salvation as does religion, or that which is simply based on habit. The family is not political, nor the exchange of goods political, nor is the relation of the follower and spiritual leader political, nor is the resort to accepting traditional authority as an imperative a political act. Kenneth Boulding separates economics from politics by saying that economics is an "unconscious" and "automatic" coordination of human activity whereas politics has the attribute of being a "conscious, rational plan of domination and subordination."[11] (Quotes are mine.) The point here is clear that it should only be the authority based on force that falls into the domain of political. Viewed as a naked force even though put into a rational-legal process, one avoids the pitfalls of looking at historical political forms long since institutionalized and accepted as emotionally as any primitive tradition. Man would be closer to a science of politics if he divested himself of a specific milieu and treated it in its semantic sense of having force, immediate or potential, to put decisions into effect, that this force has its legitimacy in claiming to restore order and when restored must disappear, or as Marx would say, "wither away." This last point, the extinction of political authority itself, is one of the most problematical parts of political authority and leads to the confusion of understanding its true function. Political authority is supposed to do its job and then, like the Arabs, fold its tent and quietly fade away until it has another obligation.

Here is the hitch: once it gains power it is reluctant to give it up just because its job is done. This is one problem that the Soviets face. Marx demanded that the state wither away as soon as its job was done but it does not give indications of doing just that. In countries like the United States, political authority may reduce itself or be forced into helplessness, but it too argues: How can we be potent the next time around? There is no purported solution for the proper levels of extinction after performing its task. The only point that needs to be drawn here is that a rational, economical decrease of authority needs to be considered in the over all evaluation of political authority if a correct assessment is to be made of what is actually happening. Treating it only as a growing thing does not put one in a position to see it when it takes on the hard form of a stable tradition of class structure, of obedience based on love or economic gain.

iii. *Political Authority Defined*

Political authority therefore must be considered as essentially a substitute authority, as an artificial authority in society. It is not the natural development of skill or professionalism that gives one the status of an expert in a given field. Nor is it genetically the parent of society as is the institution of the family. It is not a natural economic, fraternal or religious order. The political authority is created when the professions or institutions, that are natural and grow without prearranged human design, are placed in a critical position and fail to function as expected. Thus a surrogate is invented. It is never meant to be permanent and natural as are the noncoercive authorities, although in an individual's short life it may take on the appearance of permanency. Its true nature is, however, its fluidity—its contrived and dynamic substance, its interchangeable form, its coercive character, its total economy in resolving conflict.

Yet the surrogate nature of political authority is not formed out of the brow of Zeus but must be made in terms of a given social condition, and derived from that geo-social condition, and from the nature of the challenge to be faced. Thus, it must demand the highest of human inventiveness to do the job, and unfortunately cannot be made into a permanently fixed form like democracy, constitution, Marxism, royalty, etc. In times of crisis like war or economic instability, it must be able to appear, like Proteus, in the mantle most appropriate to economically perform its function and disappear when the job is done. Like adrenalin in the human body, it must be able to activate that segment which properly has to meet the danger and then must be able to retreat. We have far too little knowledge of how political authority diminishes and in what form it is most successful. Following World War II, political authority diminished in quantity in the United States but not obviously, because many of the visual though hollow trappings of power remained, especially those related to war. Lyndon Johnson's Presidency appeared as an apparent continuity of total growth of political authority, but failed to notice the degree of consensus it involved.

A far more significant loss of political authority has been occurring rather imperceptibly since the end of World War II than is apparent in the next few examples given. To appreciate this point the extent to which traditional authority has been re-emerging needs to be reconsidered. And an increase of other authorities must indicate a decrease in the political area. There is a new development of the traditional imperative that is as powerful as any that were found in the pre-industrial society. One needs no alteration of Weber's words to see that the traditional authority he described in primitive agricultural and early industrial society is back in business in our highly scientific-urban society. Weber's own words can be used in the description of traditional society and in interpreting it in a modern context.

> The organizational group exercising authority is, in the simplest case, primarily based on relations of personal loyalty, cultivated through a common process of education. The person exercising authority is not a "superior" but a personal "chief."
> His administrative staff does not consist primarily of officials, but of personal retainers . . . the chief is free to confer "grace" on the basis of his personal pleasure, his personal likes and dislikes, quite arbitrarily . . .[12]

A new order is being developed in Western Europe and Russia. It is slower in developing but this may be due to the greater changes these countries recently faced or the censorship studies of this nature would encounter. Milovan's Djilas' book, *The New Class*, regarding the communist order suggests something of the same is, nevertheless, happening.

The consequence of the preceding has some disturbing points for the study of government. It makes it a rather pointless and fruitless exercise to study the best form of government for all time, whether one does it in Plato's framework of Guardians and Philosopher Kings, or whether it be Greek Democracy by lot, or in the Jefferson-Jackson democracy by majority rule. Since the conditions demanding political authority at any given time vary, it would be sheer folly to try to force a given pattern of political authority.

The variation of political authority should be examined with regard to certain tasks which normally occupy its time. One of the prime tasks for the creation of political authority is against an outside danger. These may be many and varied. If the outside danger is a disease, then the expansion of political authority is and should be in medicine. If the outside danger is military, then the political expansion should be in the military area. The tasks of political authority internally, of group against group, conflict in values, etc., are even more varied, and attention should be on the crucial factor about political authority, its flexibility, and its adaptability and especially its method and success of extinction. The political authority on a space ship, that in the future may undertake journeys comparable to the ocean voyages of sailing vessels in the past, will need a captain with absolute power over the smallest personal activity. Yet, once space journeys are routinized, a space ship may operate like a self-service elevator with no political relationships. This change in the function and quantity of political authority is most obvious in comparing wartime periods with those of relative peace. This is true whether the War of 1812, the Civil

War, World War I, or World War II is considered. During all these periods, the function and quantity of government increased substantially in comparison to pre and post war periods.

Therefore unless there is an aberration, once the social organization attains a reasonable degree of peace and harmony in industrial society, there should be a corresponding decrease of political authority. As churches and religious organizations become more effective in setting goals there should be a corresponding decrease in political authority. As educational institutions begin to perform their role effectively, there should be a decrease in political activity. This change of interest, even now, seems apparent among the younger intellectuals who are choosing university and science careers in preference to politics.[13]

The decrease in the quantity of political authority should in no way decrease its importance as a social function and an area of study. By reducing the area of what is to be included and what excluded, a greater preciseness becomes possible. The subject is not diluted to the point where everything is eventually absorbed as legitimately a governmental function. The study should concentrate on the most economic political authority that can be utilized. Its economy must be measured in terms of minimum resources necessary to fulfill what should be considered a lapse in social continuity. The activity must be able to automatically increase in power when necessary and decrease with equal efficiency. Once viewed this way, it may be possible to dissociate political authority with the ideological attachments that it has assumed in the last hundred years. It should not be thought of as democratic or dictatorial authority but rather as efficient or inefficient.

Notes: Chapter 7

1. H. H. Gerth and C. Wright Mills, *From Max Weber: Essays,* New York, Oxford University Press, 1946, pp. 77–78.
2. Peter Odegard, et al., *American Government,* New York, Holt, Rinehart, and Winston, 1961 (See Chapter 1).
3. Ibid., p. 3.
4. The use of the word "public" does not imply a necessity of wide dissemination as would be the case in the United States. It is used here in the sense that nothing is considered private from Soviet political power.
5. See especially Weber's *Theory of Social and Economic Organization,* Glencoe, Ill., The Free Press, 1947.
6. For our purpose Weber's charismatic authority category which performs the function of catalyst from traditional to legal authority is useful and not in question here.
7. Everett Hagen, *On The Theory of Social Change,* Homewood, Ill., The Dorsey Press, 1962, pp. 57–58.
8. Joseph LaPolambara, ed., *Bureaucracy and Political Development,* Princeton, Princeton University Press, 1963, p. 5.
9. Victor Thompson, *Modern Organization,* New York, Alfred A. Knopf, 1963, p. 11.
10. David Easton, *The Political System,* New York, Alfred A. Knopf, 1953, p. 129.
11. Kenneth Boulding, *The Organizational Revolution,* New York, Harper Brothers, 1953, p. 49.
12. Max Weber, *Theory of Social and Economic Organization,* Glencoe, Ill., The Free Press, 1947, pp. 341–43.
13. David Bell, *End of Ideology,* New York, Collier Books, 1961, p. 39.

8. THE RE-SURGENCE OF CLASS AS AN INDICATION OF STABILITY

i. *Equalitarianism: The Spirit of the Revolutionary Period*

One of the most cherished values of the Revolutionary period was Equality. It was the idea that one man is as good as another—not just good in the eyes of God, but also in the eyes of his fellow man here on earth. In the initial stages of the advocacy of equality a great English theorist Thomas Hobbes used the arguments of physical science to demonstrate equality. In his *Leviathan,* Hobbes treated the human being as a physical object. One person, he held, was relatively the same weight, or took the same space as another. At least, there was no evidence to Hobbes that a person of royalty occupied more space than one of common birth. Nor was there any indication to him that one man was significantly stronger than another. He saw that the weakest of men was capable of killing the strongest, which demonstrated to him the equality of men.

Another of the great English theorists who gave birth and succor to the idea of equality was John Locke. He helped to promote the idea of mental equality, and the belief of human equality at birth. Locke wrote that the mind of man at birth was a wax tablet, a *tabula rasa,* on which impressions were made from the individual's experiences. The explanation for the wiser among us was due to the greater amount of experience impressions that had been made on our wax brain and not to royal birth. These literary and logical presentations of equality charged through the American and French Revolutions like a fire through a very dry forest. They gave a rationale and an inspiration to all the critics of the old order of aristocracy by birth. They claimed that such distinctions were built upon false premises and sustained by deceit.

With the criticism of hereditary aristocracy came the logical suspicion of all assertions of earthly superiority. In a highly equalitarian and individualistic society such as ours a great deal of human comparison could be avoided. The obvious differences between people which could not be obscured, such as distinctions of poverty and wealth, were strangely enough not credited to the individual but to God.[1] All pride in individual accomplishments over those of his fellow men were treated as the greatest of human vices. And hereditary aristocracy was the visible establishment of this source of evil in the world. It had to be destroyed.

The destruction of hereditary aristocracy still based on the agricultural-provincial order proceeded rapidly in those countries where the urban-universal revolution was under way. For here the functions of the old aristocracy were being eliminated, and their answers to problems faced by industrial man were neither productive nor meaningful. The formulae for the good life did not apply. To talk in the Tolstoyan sense about the wonders of nature, the beauty of the countryside, friendship, respect for the elders, obedience by children, all meaningful to the farmer, were empty to the coalminer whose whole family had to work, either in mines or in enclosed factories to stay alive. The miner's family may be under several bosses, none of whom may have cared about his workers. "What countryside?" the miner asked. What loyalty from the children? Where were the undying friendships? D. H. Lawrence's *Sons and Lovers* and *Lady Chatterly's Lover* well illustrate this despondency of the urban individual and the helplessness of the aristocracy. It must be pointed out again that it was not aristocracy per se that was so out of tune with the times but an aristocracy that was based on the agricultural-provincial structure of society which by the nineteenth century was rapidly falling apart to the thrusts of the new industrial order. (See Chapter 3 for a fuller discussion of this point.)

The tendency to oversimplify social problems is evident in all social movements where popular support is necessary. Thus the problems of hunger, starvation, misery, unemployment, war, vice, and all the petty hatreds that grew up between the people in their relationships with each other were all directed at the scapegoat of inequality. The attack was based on all levels from political inequality through social, economic, educational, down to the more nebulous psychological inequality.

The destruction of the hereditary aristocracy and its variation in other forms was the death knell of the traditional agriculturally based authorities and, as already indicated in an earlier chapter, the rise of political authority. The battle cry was for a return to a more natural state of life in this world, without aristocratic airs of superiority and inferences of inferiority, without privilege and rank. This new equality would purportedly return man to the supposed idyllic "state of nature" that became so prominent in the nineteenth century. The Garden of

Eden, the people were told, provided no discrimination between humans in terms of ability or potential. The couplet of the time was:

> When Adam delved and Eve span
> Where was then the Gentleman?

This battle against the old traditional authority produced some of the greatest critical literature of our history. Interestingly enough, as H. L. Mencken recalls in his *Notes on Democracy,* it was usually the creation of disenchanted aristocrats, or those commoners brought up in aristocracy but without the legitimacy to the tradition of rank. Montesquieu, Voltaire and Rousseau led the attack. There were the less literary, and less legitimate, like Tom Paine in America, who nevertheless were probably more effective in their own time in bringing down the house of agricultural-provincial authority than were any of the great literati. The literature in defense of equality never matched that in opposition to hereditary aristocracy. Nevertheless, the ideas were believed and adopted wherever they were propagated. They were the "flying wedge" of the urban-universal revolution. They recruited the ranks for the armies against the agricultural-provincial civilization.

The mid-nineteenth century finally spawned an effective democrat against all privilege, against all inequality, the champion of the masses, Karl Marx. He was to provide the program and the methods in the name of science which promised to destroy all private property, the source of all inequality and aristocracy and their middle-class followers which he called bourgeois. With words he incited the non-aristoi to rise immediately and to attack violently all rank and privilege, all inequality. What the final fruits of such a war would be Marx never spent time to visualize. He helped bring down the house of rural order. How humans were permanently to live in the city without lust, avarice, and vice, Marx only indicated by assuming that everything was caused by the aristocratic myth, and equality given a real opportunity would demonstrate itself.[2]

ii. *The Three Great Revolutions of the Revolutionary Period*

The United States as a nation was in the best position to embellish and implement the hopes of an equalitarian civilization. Three million settlers had won a struggle against the most powerful aristocracy then in existence. Amateur armies beat professional soldiers. Primitive manufacturers defeated time-tested craftsmanship. Ignorant, illiterate men triumphed over the educated and sophisticated. Was this not proof that traditional authority was a great fraud? It was also apparent, not only to Americans but to aristocrats like Alexis de Tocqueville, that the democrats given a real opportunity could become highly productive as was being demonstrated in America. The benefits it received from England and other Western European nations which permitted it to proceed rapidly were considered irrelevant. The natural abundance of the American continent itself was also treated as irrelevant. America characterized equality, and as de Tocqueville believed, it was the wave of the future. That it was in reality a destroyer of the past is to precede the train of development.

In 1829 de Tocqueville came to America to view the country that was then most advanced in equalitarian democracy. He hoped to learn certain lessons that might preserve the best aspects of an aristocracy. While he saw the equalitarian force as irresistible, it was not necessarily all-pervasive to the total exclusion of aristocracy. There was still hope as de Tocqueville foresaw, for a preservation of the best aspects of aristocracy, provided it could learn the lessons that prompted equality.

De Tocqueville was correct. There was a place in the world for a ranking of people on the basis of talent, performance, etc. There was also a place for heredity to function as a factor in organizing society because children are likely to resemble their parents, and be educated and helped by their parents. But as long as conditions were in a revolutionary flux there was little opportunity for this to operate. Aristocracy could not be vital again until the times became more stable. The period of the great political revolutions was not such a time. Beginning with the American Revolution of 1776 through the French in 1789, the Russian in 1917, and the continuing ones in the undeveloped countries of the world there had been little opportunity for the development of a new traditional authority.

The American, French and Russian revolutions were the violent and local demonstrations of this new force which signalled the death of agriculturally based aristocracy, and the rise of political authority. The American Revolution which came first announced to the world that people opposed to the old traditional authority had a right to revolt—that a nation could be organized on political authority alone, i.e., rationality and compulsion. The past would count for nothing and only present performance would be the criteria on which people would act and be judged. This was formalized in the Declaration of Independence as all men being created equal and implied that they should have equal participation regardless of hered-

itary background. Religious, traditional, intellectual, artistic authority fell to the new political authority formalized in majority rule. Fortunately the aspirations fell far
short of the goal or else we would have had a barbaric
society. The residue of traditional authority continued to
hold most people, even though it was rapidly decaying,
while the new political authority made decisions and gave
direction which lay a basis for a new tradition. It is little
wonder that de Tocqueville found little real freedom for
the individual in America, actually less than under the
old traditional society.

The French Revolution a few years later attempted to
put an end to rural traditional authority. It performed
the same function as did the American Revolution and in
the long run with considerably less political authority. It
appeared more vicious in its early stages because it was
more of a civil war than the American. Also, in the early
stages the political authority in the form of Napoleon appeared more naked and inhuman. However, in a short
time Napoleon recognized that pure power could not last.
He would be the next victim as had been the Dantons
and Robespierres. So he compromised and relented his
attack on the traditional authorities. His power, however,
was always potentially threatening, and this forced the
aristocracy to continue to adjust to the physical and
mental revolution taking place. Thus political authority
after Napoleon never played the role it did in the United
States and the U.S.S.R.

The Russian Revolution was a prime example of nearly
total victory of political power over traditional authority.
It demonstrated more sharply than the preceding two, a
total physical and mental revolution, and the place political authority plays in revolution. It was also more in-

human, more barbaric, and the final escape from this barbarism did not begin to take place until new traditional authorities began to reemerge. The urban-universal revolution in Russia is still less certain, less assured since political authority is still so powerful, and it certainly will not liquidate itself contrary to what Marx believed. The Soviet performance in this respect is therefore of great interest to other pre-revolutionary nations. Can political authority perform all the functions of life for a while, give birth to a new nonpolitical tradition and then commit suicide in a short span of time, or will it persist at the expense of the development of more natural authority and in fact delay the urban-universal civilization for a time?

iii. *Science: The New Base For Aristocracy*

Regardless of the route taken by the various agricultural-provincial civilizations to the urban-universal the result on arrival is an apparent decline of political authority. Since stability requires rank and order there is a corresponding decline of general equality. Furthermore, the nature of the new urban-universal world is itself contradictory to equality, especially the scientific aspect of the revolution.

Let us examine two works on this problem of the relationship of equality to science: Henry Alonzo Myers' book *Are Men Equal* and Alfred North Whitehead's *Science and the Modern World*. Both were published immediately after World War II. Both books are considered authoritative statements in the discussion of their particular subject. Neither of the two authors examine whether science and equality are compatible or contradictory, but read together they raise an important question about the relationship of these two areas. First Myers accuses the Germans of the period of Hitler's *Mein Kampf* and the preceding period of German history of falling prey to inequality, the belief in superiority of their race. In this manner Myers goes on to explain how the doctrine of inequality led to barbarism, and how it has always led to tragedy.

Now let us look at Whitehead's book which attempts to explain where science first developed and some of the characteristics associated with it. While Whitehead gives the English the credit for modern technology, and putting it into practice, the Germans are given credit for first realizing in the recent period the importance of science on a general scale. He says of the Germans:

> They abolished haphazard methods of scholarship. In their technological schools and universities progress did not have to wait for the occasional genius, or the occasional lucky thought. Their feats of scholarship during the nineteenth century were the admiration of the world. This discipline of knowledge applies beyond technology to pure science, and beyond science to general scholarship. It represents the change from amateurs to professionals.[3]

Did the Germans choose inequality or did they choose science, scholarship, professionalism, science and their fruits, i.e., high production of material goods? Could they have chosen science wthout inequality? The answer will remain debatable. It does demonstrate, however, that inequality and science were compatible, and perhaps more than that, science actually encourages rank and professionalism.

While choosing science does not mean the choice of superiority in ethnical areas, it certainly does mean superiority or professionalism in technical areas if one is to be scientific. It means making objective distinctions between individuals of various specializations, emphasizing their different skills, tasks and roles, ranking them, increasing precision control and quality.

The rise of the urban-universal world to predominance does not mean the total eclipse of equality as a continuing factor in our way of life, any more than the revolutionary equalitarian movement was able to totally eclipse rural aristocracy and its manifest variations in superiority and excellence. It does mean that in a stable urban-universal world class and privilege will play a much greater role, and that decisions at all social, political and economic levels are more likely to be made by a professional in authority than by the amateur or an incidental group through majority rule.

Questioning equality as a continuing vital force in our lives will appear to be questioning all democratic values. Let me remind the reader that equality and political democracy are not identical, even though some would interpret them as such. Democracy means participation in government by the people, but that participation does not have to be equal to everyone else's participation. While some democrats would contend that democracy becomes meaningless for them without equalitarian action they omit the democracies that functioned with class and rank. For democracy in a consent aspect is not threatened by the urban-universal world, even though in its egalitarian aspect it faces what appear to be insurmountable obstacles. The ancient Greeks it must be remembered combined democracy with slavery. Aristotle concluded after his pragmatic study of Greek constitutions that a polity was the best form of government. His polity did not deny the existence of classes but did provide participation and responsibility for all classes. In more modern times we find democracies still functioning with hereditary monarchies. We find democracies without the right of franchise for women. We find democracies that use age and literacy as conditions affecting the franchise. One can make a good case for a non-egalitarian democracy from the philosophies of John Adams, Alexander Hamilton, or even Thomas Jefferson and remain in the framework of democracy in America. Walter Lippmann's book *The Public Philosophy* does essentially this for the current period. The professional leader has responsibilities and obligations that he has to meet even if the amateur is ignorant of them.

My questioning the vitality of egalitarianism is not pejorative but rather as a consequence of stability and increased specialization. Equality, especially in the performance of a job, regardless of the intensity of the desire to do it, is no substitute for talent and training in a highly urbanized society. Specialization is vital to science and has been basic in accounting for the industrial boon. It is an anathema to a leveling of standards in order that most may be able to perform the specialized activity. Imagine reducing highly specialized engineering or surgery to a "do it yourself" level of a twelve-year-old. It cannot be done without putting in the skilled work beforehand. When the majority of the American people were farmers, their relation to each other and the state could be handled in a uniform manner. But the responsibilities of specialized and professional people to their occupations, to research, to each other and to the state are different in character in the urban-universal world. The police, in their professional capacity, have a responsibility substantially different from that of the doctor of medicine, the nuclear physicist, the college teacher, the architect, the airplane pilot, the janitor, the truck driver, or a United States Senator. These are the skills demanded in lieu of farming. When these people act qua their professional occupation which occupies the major portion of their day, their obligations and responsibilities are different and their legal responsibilities are different, and their rewards have to be of a different nature. Thus the leveling of standards becomes increasingly difficult to apply as the areas of specialization are further proliferated and professionalized. And an examination of occupations today reveals to us the rapid decrease of jobs not requiring specialized training.

There appears to be little likelihood of any return to a hereditary aristocracy, but even one of the most fought for beliefs of equality, that of no social distinction, has lost supporters. In order to extract from all professions the full effort necessary for the function of our urban-universal society, we have been forced to offer incentives beyond the more egalitarian one of money. We are forced, as are the Soviets, to offer the more aristocratic social distinctions of honor, i.e., the honor of being a scientist, and the Nobel or other awards beyond the monetary that provide incentive. The same is being done in the other professions, those closest to the queen of the sciences, physics, down to the less scientific professions. Thus a non-hereditary social aristocracy is evident and increasingly more necessary as urbo-industrialism raises its performance requirements to the level where high morale is vital. We can still save a vital part of equality which is consistent with specialization, the "equality of opportunity." This can permit the structuring of elites and classes on the basis of performance and has a basis in our heritage through Jefferson.

In our previous equalitarian orientation we put the emphasis on the similarity of man. We took the Hobbesian description of the nature of man being of a rather uniform variety which took for its example that the weakest man could kill the strongest. We followed this in America with a Jacksonian tenet that the occupations of this earth, including the political tasks, could be performed by nearly anyone. Most of our social sciences, especially in America, took the assumption that poor performance on anyone's part was an environmental rather than a genetic factor, and when the genetic factor was recognized it was neglected as of insignificant consideration as prescription for social organization. We always knew that there were differences in performance which no amount of environmental variation could alter. But it was easier to flow with the equalitarian tide of history and so we favored studies which supported our ethic rather than those that challenged it. We could afford this levelling in the early stages of the urban-universal civilization but it is too costly in a mature and stable urban-universal society. These small, by our previous standards, variations in individuals make the difference between high level of performance and stability of inefficiency and instability. Take for example the performance of the select group of astronauts nurtured and trained in the Soviet Union and America. One tenth of a second reflex advantage by one person over another may be sufficient variation to provide for a successful performance or a costly failure. Or consider the select group working on atomic projects. These differences will become more acute as our urban-universal civilization expands. We will not be able to spend and waste twenty-five years on a psychiatrist or nuclear physicist when his stamina, motivation, or intelligence may falter for his crucial years of work. We will not be able to afford the luxury, especially in our educational institutions, of obscuring the differences. Thus intellectual and academic levelling in our emerging urban-universal world would be too disruptive and unstabling, not in a progressive sense, but in a regressive sense.

In countries where psychologically and socially the idea of aristocracy had not disappeared to any great extent, as in the countries of Western and northern Europe, the elimination of the unstable elements of equality, especially its arrogance against professional pride may be accomplished with little disturbance.

The vital book in England in 1929 was Tawney's *Equality;* thirty years later in 1961 the vital book in England was Young's *Meritocracy* which reversed the thesis. The following quotes expose this transition.

> *Equality:* It may well be the case that capricious inequalities are in some measure inevitable, in the sense that, like crime and disease, they are a malady which the most rigorous precautions cannot wholly overcome. But, when crime is known as crime, and disease as disease, the ravages of both are circumscribed by the mere fact that they are recognized for what they are, and described by their proper names, not by flattering euphemisms. And a society which is convinced that inequality is an evil need not be alarmed because the evil is one which cannot wholly be subdued. In recognizing the poison it will have armed itself with an antidote. It will have deprived inequality of its sting by stripping it of its esteem.[4]

> *The Rise of the Meritocracy 1870–2033:* Exceptional brains require exceptional teaching: Russians and

Americans could not see it. They forced every child to do what he was not good at as well as at what he was. By showing that all men are equally duffers at something—what could be more easy?—they went as far as they could to show that no man is a genius at anything —what could be more dangerous? In the name of equality they wantonly sacrificed the few to the many. . . . Englishmen of the solid centre never believed in equality. They assumed that some men were better than others, and only waited to be told in what respect. Equality? Why, there would be no one to look up to any more. Most Englishmen believed, however dimly, in a vision of excellence which was part and parcel of their own time-honoured aristocratic tradition. It was because of this that the campaign for comprehensive schools failed. It was because of this that we have our modern society: by imperceptible degrees an aristocracy of birth has turned into an aristocracy of talent.[5]

The vital book in America which followed Young's *Meritocracy* in England with essentially the same thesis but with a more circumspect approach which we might expect was John W. Gardner's *Excellence—Can We Be Equal And Excellent Too? The Christian Science Monitor* review of it stated: "Once in a while a book comes along which, if taken to heart, possesses the capacity to lift the whole tone of a nation's thinking. John W. Gardner has produced such a book."

A significant quote from the book which summarizes Gardner's thesis follows:

Standards! That is a word for every American to write on his bulletin board. We must face the fact that there are a good many things in our character and in our national life which are inimical to standards—laziness, complacency, the desire for a fast buck, the American fondness for short cuts, reluctance to criticize slackness, to name only a few. Every thinking American knows in his heart that we must sooner or later come to terms with these failings.[6]

The mass democratic movements of these same countries by going to extremes did little credit to equality. The communist defenders of equality showed it in its worst elements. The United States never witnessed comparable demonstrations of the masses in this country, and on the other hand the aristocratic, professional orientation was never strong. Thus the pursuit of "excellence" in contrast to the pursuit of "equality" may be more difficult to be realized. This also applies to the Soviet Union. However, if Gardner's book on excellence and the various elite studies in the United States are indicative of what is happening, the transition from an equalitarian to a class society has already taken place. It has been circumspect and unannounced, but it is nevertheless there and functioning.

Yet without the outward signs and manifestations of respect that these elites need they are likely to respond to more base compensations than is good for a class system. If the only rewards of any significance will continue to be those of egalitarian wealth and political power the functions of a superior class will not be performed without a substantial amount of crass and barbarism. Thus the ameliorating influences on an aristocracy of talent must be as vital as those which in America worked so beneficially on the egalitarian period of our history. These are well described in de Tocqueville's *Democracy in America*. It will probably take another foreigner to describe accurately our "new class" period of history.

Notes: Chapter 8

1. Calvinistic Christianity, which according to Max Weber's *Protestant Ethic* and R. H. Tawney's *Religion and The Rise of Capitalism*, had a strong influence on Christianity in America, was very conscious of economic distinctions. However, curiously enough they altered the previous Christian position of equality before God to an already determined inequality before God over which the individual no longer had any control. Thus the individual here on earth was helpless over such differences as economic inequality.

2. It is litle wonder that democrats since have had a guilty conscience. While they agreed with Marx on equality, they hesitated at such extreme and violent measures. The mass democratic equalitarian movements of the thirties in Europe and America appalled enough to start as vigorous a flight to the opposite extreme, inequality—the inequality of races, nations and talents so obviously championed by Hitler's Germany and Mussolini's Italy. Yet both eventually prepared the route for a new authority of tradition, peaceful, lawful and based on a functional talent.

3. Alfred N. Whitehead, *Science and the Modern World*, New York, Macmillan, 1953, pp. 98–99.

4. Richard Tawney, *Equality*, New York, Harcourt, Brace, 1931, pp. 48–49.

5. Michael Young, *The Rise of the Meritocracy*, Baltimore, Md., Penguin Books, 1961, pp. 45–49.

6. John W. Gardner, *Excellence*, New York, Harper Colophon Books, 1961, pp. 158–159.

Part III
The Urban-Universal As
Our New Home

9. THE SPHERE OF CREATIVITY

i. *Man the Inventor*

Nothing in history so aptly distinguishes man from
other animals as the power to be creative. Other animal
species can in may ways outdo man, e.g., running, fighting,
loyalty, bravery, and even memory, but none compares
to man's genius to take nearly anything of this world and
transform it into something else. Man prides himself on
his creative power, makes his gods extremely capable at
creativity and ennobles those of his species who show the
greatest skill in creativity. Neither the form of social
organization nor personal condition has ever existed for
any length of time where this characteristic was absent.
Men in prisons under the most deprived conditions manage to write poems, domesticate animals or find ingenious
ways of deceiving their keepers. We do not have to go
into the question of whether prison conditions, or political
totalitarian conditions tend to be less conducive to creativity than man with more options. The answer would
undoubtedly be that the person or society with more options will be more creative (all other things being equal).
The point is that man tends to be creative regardless of
the nature of his conditions.

The question for the reader to comprehend is what
happens to this human in a state where the urban-universal
revolution has ended. The only answer can be that man
will continue to be just as creative, or perhaps more so,

while at the same time maintaining a stability, an order to his life. To appreciate this apparent contradiction between creativity and stability, we must reconsider creativity in different manifestations. Creativity is not a fixed entity. It is a force which must burst out of humans, but this force does not have to end in the construction of a cathedral, a factory, more bushels of grain, or guided missiles. It is true that during the revolutionary period its manifestations in physical production, in quantity, were the prime bases for measuring a person's creativity, his worth. It was not of great consequence that one ran his neighbor out of business, neglected his children, destroyed his health, caused conflict; the main question that had to be answered was, how much did he produce materially.

Since the ethic of a stable urban-universal world is not on production, but on order, the honors for creativity will go to those who can be creative in these areas. The question which will have to be answered will not be in production but on whether one's force, one's effort leads to more or less stability. One of the great American social theorists, Thorstein Veblen, made us well aware of the extent to which personal activity is directed, by emphasizing those things that the social system honors. If the society esteems physical power then the effort will be made in that direction. If it esteems money then craftsmanship will be subordinated to wealth. In his *Theory of the Leisure Class* he shows that leisure is not valid for itself in a pecuniary society but only as an indication of pecuniary consumption, i.e., the ability to refrain from work for which there is pecuniary compensation, or as Veblen in his inimitable style says, "conspicuous abstention from labor therefore becomes the conventional work of superior pecuniary achievement and the conventional index and reputability . . ."[1] It is an interesting phenomenon that one of the most physically dynamic developments in the United States, the federal urban renewal program, is increasingly subscribing to a philosophy of maintaining equilibrium in the community in renewal. Every effort at change will now consider the total consequences to the entire community by the projected proposal. Earlier, under the production ethic the problem seemed simpler. An old dilapidated house would be replaced by a new one; a slum neighborhood was sufficient reason for its being razed. Now the new must fit in with the old and if it does not, it is the new that is more likely to be retarded.

Perhaps the most meaningful fact about creativity in an urban-universal world will be its direction into different channels, requiring just as much ingenuity but limiting physical productivity. The brainpower of America may be siphoned off from the technical engineering areas and directed to the psychological areas. It can take a psychiatrist just as much brainpower to establish a harmonious relationship between two people, and be as demanding and creative of his energy as it did for George Westinghouse to perfect the air brake. It can take as much creativity for a diplomat to devise a plan to prevent war as it took for Nobel to produce dynamite. Thus, it should be clearly apparent that creativity can be extensive without being materially productive. Some areas into which creative energy might readily flow in the urban-universal world could be fruitfully examined.

ii. *The Forms of Creativity*

The area that most forcefully comes to mind as one requiring a great deal of creative talent is one of international conflict. There is an extensive desire among urbanized nations to find formulae to prevent war and maintain peace. The production of more cars, more clothes or more food is simply a matter of investment. It is primarily a matter of refining technology. The person who does this innovation is materially rewarded but he no longer is considered the hero of society. But the innovators for peace and stability in the world can now expect the honor of being the great celebrities. It is not an easy task and the competitors for these honors will find the competition tough and demanding. The United Nations was a brilliant innovation. It may be the prototype for the future or a blind alley as many a direction in industry. The Common Market and the American Peace Corps are as demanding of creativity, initiative, drive, as any Copernicus or Columbus.

Another area that forcefully comes to mind in a highly urbanized world is the tendency for technology, and especially one phase of it, automation, to put humans out of their traditional jobs. It will take a great creative effort to reorient people from a work life of material production to a life of education or of service to others. While leisure might traditionally have required little attention because there was so little of it, it now may demand the most extensive attention because there is so much of it. To use one's leisure time significantly may thus require the highest level of effort by a great number of people. Olympic games and various sports associations will bid for the best people, for those who can use their bodies in ways never contemplated by man.

A third area equally as demanding in non-materially oriented creativity is man's health. Never before have we put such a high price on human health, both physical and psychological. It is at present hard to conceive of any great variation in the human specie, especially in the length of life or in ability to adapt. Within the present framework there is, nevertheless, an opportunity for millions of ingenious people to make millions of contributions to the lives of people. Many of the present ills will be eliminated or alleviated. The opportunity for talent is unlimited.

Finally, the area which may demand the highest skills and highest creativity is the spiritual. The world feels itself spiritually bankrupt and this is basically true. It has been sharply called to our attention by philosophers like Søren Kierkegaard to the more applicable like Harvey Cox in *The Secular City* who claim the gods of traditional religion have been unseated. They recognize the need for the most challenging type of creativity that needs to take place. The secular city, the urban-universal world will have its own peculiar style and demands. The answers to its problems, the integration of its whole life which is the proper function of religion will have a mountainous task to perform. It is not unrealistic to look for a second coming of Christ. How and when he will appear, and how he will be treated, only future generations will know when they can look on it historically.

These examples only scratch the surface of a great flood of creativity that can be directed toward order. As soon as one goes beyond the individual and his interpersonal contacts one enters another realm of social ordering, the group and the nation. The area of civil rights is a current investment in creativity that the United States has selected as a prime concern. A great number of resources, energy, can be used in creative ways to disestablish one order and to establish another. Another area of prime concern for the United States is the education of all its

citizens to the highest potential possible. This will undoubtedly involve the most inventive and ingenious
methods ever conceived by man. Yet the consequences of
this are not to expect more television sets or more high-
rise buildings, but rather a respect for other people and
a respect for one's own worth. More time may be spent
by a highly educated person in the appreciation of a walk
through a forest or in listening to an opera than in producing more doorknobs.

Perhaps one of the greatest celebrated virtues and also
liabilities of the revolutionary period was the anonymity
of the individual. With the continual break-up of the
social ties of the agricultural world, plus the emphasis on
production the individual found a release, a freedom from
others in various ways. For those interested in a fresh start
in life, a wiping clean of the slate regarding earlier behavior and indiscretions, the revolutionary period provided maximum opportunities. On the other hand, it also
brought a social callousness toward the sufferings from
anomy, of the failing to re-establish social relations when
they tired of anonymity. The post-revolutionary period
is rapidly decreasing the opportunities of asocial, or
anomic individuals just as was the case in the agricultural
civilization. Every individual's actions will be of social
concern, and an ethic supporting this is being formulated.
The physical controls to support this ethic will be in the
records that are kept and in the social realization that
a single anomic individual may be a threat to the entire
social mechanism.

The new self will be hammered out on the anvil of a
tight interpersonal world. Identity will not be a problem,
at least no more than it ever was in the past. What will
be different is the framework in which identity will be

formed. Traditional concepts of identity highly successful to an agricultural world will be poor guides for new identities. The traditional identities of the male and female role will be significantly altered. The parent-child roles and those of close relatives will have little resemblance to their place in agricultural society.

The new roles will not fall with equal weight. For some the new opportunity for self-development will be greater than ever before and they will move into their roles with eagerness. The reverse will be true for others. Perhaps the most difficult one for adjustment will be the young male. He will suffer the most significant diminution of power-to-act. The rural-provincial world was built upon the family unit and generally the most valuable member for survival and prosperity of that unit was the male between the ages of sixteen and fifty. Where brute strength was a crucial arbiter of production, justice, and revenge, it was inevitable that the mature male predominate. The women, children, and the aged, probably, ninety percent of the social structure, were subordinate to the mature and virile male. It is in this respect that the urban-universal world is castrating his power, glory, and freedom to act. It is he who may be the most resentful of his role in the urban-universal world.

It is going to be difficult for the male to accept that survival and justice in the urban-universal world are products of technology and science and the basis of allocating role will not be on brute strength but on the fact of being a human being, male, female, young and old. Issues of authority will exist but they will be without regard to the different categories but rather structured in terms of the job performed.

The occupations which will almost entirely be in the

human service areas will involve the women and the aged in equal capacity to the young male. The primary occupations will be as teachers, doctors, lawyers, politicians, entertainers and a small number of plant maintenance workers. The women, children and aged will substantially outnumber the mature males in these areas.

With physical productivity performed by automated machinery in our urban-universal world of the near future, productive work which is seldom creative, will naturally take less of an individual's time. As indicated earlier, most people will simply be changing occupations from the productive to the service areas. The majority of these service occupations will be less monotonous and less dangerous. They will be able to call on various categories of our population without discrimination. And when discrimination occurs it is as likely to be against the young male as it might be in his favor. This resentment will manifest itself in some final but abortive efforts at physical violence demonstrations.

With the economy of machinery for material production there will be more opportunity to individualize social service, and thus, in fact, a greater opportunity will arise for personal creativity. Teaching, whether golf, tennis or philosophy, is a good example of reasonably creative opportunity for self expression through service. The same is true in medicine or the entertainment world. Yet in all these cases the immediate fruits are not in more production but in more extensive use of products. Thus, creativity in the urban-universal world is bound to remain as intense as it is in a revolutionary world of great economic and physical change, but that creativity will have a new form. At first it will be socially sought after in the large social and spiritual adjustments that have to follow.

Secondly, it will be on the individual basis as man always has to establish his identity, and place in the world. This identity will be in the contributions to art and intellect rather than to price and product.

Note: Chapter 9

1. Thorstein Veblen, *The Theory of the Leisure Class*, Mentor Books, 1953, p. 43.

10. THE SPHERE OF LEARNING AND THE SCHOOLS OF THE FUTURE

i. *The Place of the New Learning*

The cathedral was the symbol of civilization based on agriculture; the market place emerged as the symbol of the revolutionary period and the university is now emerging as the symbol of our new urban-universal world. The spiritual life gave way to the restless spirit of the technological innovators and commercial entrepreneurs who must in turn surrender to those who would spend their lives in the "cathedrals of learning," the giant universities, studying, researching, and learning. The university, the college, the public high school—in fact, all schools today, are the dynamos of the new order. Wherever universities are located, by virtue of their outlook, they are not provincial, nor national. Their student bodies and their faculties are already the microcosms of the new order. To live on a university campus today is to experience the life, the activity, the values and the make-up of the entire world of tomorrow.

Schools in the most urbanized countries have already taken over the direction of their respective constituents. They are in America the greatest enterprise, involve the majority of the population in giving or receiving education. They logically elicit the greatest amount of money although presently less than proportionate to the value involved in education. They are rapidly moving to a condition which will commit the greateset percentage of our lives and resources to education.

Learning and research have been recently associated with productivity. They were bred in the revolutionary period with the assumption that the learned earned the most money and were anxious to employ their education to materially productive pursuits. This assumption can no longer be treated as valid. Learning has begun, once again, to be treated as a virtue in itself and not for what use can be made of it. This attitude of an intrinsic value to education is a historical one. However, until now it was always limited to a very small minority. With life assured comfortably, the student has become increasingly eager to be a student for the rest of his life. The highest achievement is to be continuing one's education, and to remain curious and responsive to new knowledge. While education and self-realization was the only criteria of success for the small minority, it now pervades the great majority in this country. A new generation is now maturing that increasingly subscribes to this educational ethic rather than to judging the function of education by material productivity and monetary accumulation which was a product of the revolutionary period.

ii. *Higher Education as the Core of Urbanism, or the Coming of University Cities*

Higher education since World War II has become the fastest-growing industry in the American city. It remains, however, largely unrecognized because of a long tradition of its irrelevance to national politics, especially in America. In order that we might appreciate this change, we need to compare the investment in higher education today with that of the turn of the century.

Campbell Stewart, in chapter 26 of *The American College,* edited by Nevitt Sanford, traces the relative increases of population and public high school enrollment showing that between 1870 and 1955 the population of the United States increased four times, while its public high school population increased eighty times.[1] As for higher education, we see a jump in enrollment from 4 percent of young people aged eighteen to twenty-one in 1900, to 35 percent in 1964, and still climbing.[2]

In putting this in an economic perspective, it was estimated that by 1960 the production, distribution and consumption of "knowledge" in all forms accounted for 29 percent of the gross national product and that its rate of growth was about twice as fast as the rest of the economy.[3] David Riesman, one of the major students of higher education refers to universities as "the major growth industry."[4] Thus, the sheer size of the direct investment is itself staggering, much less the leadership function which is being assigned to the universities in the coming period.

Yet this numerical growth is only one segment of their economic power. The production impact on the city's economy is extensive. According to Clark Kerr, once president of the gigantic University of California, in his book *The Uses of the University,* the large majority of the government defense contracts in 1961 went to areas in part because they were "centers of learning." He also points out that the new "multiversities" as he coined them are being dangled as bait in front of prospective industries with apparently a drawing power "greater than low taxes or cheap labor."[5] Thus, education as an industry today sharply contrasts with education which is only intellectually functional.

American higher education at the turn of the century was still a classical education. It taught one to be conversant with the Greeks and Romans in their own language. The truly educated person was one who loved this dialogue with the ancients for its intrinsic worth and not because it had any relationship to the contemporary period. This was not true of the lower years of public schooling, where reading, writing and arithmetic were essential tools for the industrial society. Nor was it true of the technical and professional schools spawned by the Land Grant Act of 1862. These were highly related to the agricultural and industrial society. But they played a very subordinate role in higher education even though they were of value to agriculture and industry. They were practical schools and not oriented to research and sciences. Most of all, they were helpless pawns of political and social organizations. State governments treated the administrative posts as part of their petty patronage, and the professors were "hired hands." The dominant class in society had not accepted them as essential to their existence or growth.

The urban-universal revolution in higher education in America began at the end of the last century. Initiating this revolution which broke the classic tradition were the elective system and the development of graduate education. The elective system introduced new subjects, mostly scientifically oriented. Graduate work magnified the specialization already emphasized by science. The combination of the two put education at the head of industrial innovation and organization. They would open up the gates of new products, new architecture, new human relations, and they would organize, direct, and channel their growth. And when growth and change threatened their authority they would head the science of social order and limited growth, which really is the basis for the end of revolution.

The rationale of the classical education had been the study of Greek and Roman society to free the provincial mind from its local bias. The arguments of the new subjects of science and social science were that students would be freed from provincial bias more quickly with greater relevance to their society by learning about altering their status quo. This movement emerged in the victory of the sciences and social sciences over the classics. Departments of chemistry, biology, physics, anthropology, sociology, economics, and political science, unknown in most schools earlier, were added. These new subjects, at first revolutionary, subsequently are scholarship and subjects for erudition and the creation of the "good" and stable society.

Practical research which until the twentieth century was for all purposes still conducted by the enterprising individual in his own home, in the business establishments, and in industrial laboratories was rapidly accepted and shifted into the new university. After World War II there was an avalanche of criticism regarding the gradual erosion of the "ivory tower" education to the new "Mammon," but the educational administrator and the practical scholar (Clark Kerr called him an entrepreneur) found a new power in the business world that kept them asking for more without much worry about the consequences. The new dimension which industrial society was asking of research, especially in its quantity and cost, made it economical to have such centrally located laboratories to conduct this research. Government, private business and industry created a flood of resources moving to the university campuses. This was especially true of the federal government after World War II. Thus, if the traditional "ivy" college was not ready to sacrifice its purity, the new "city universities" were there, willing to corrupt themselves with research on the "transistor" or "polio." The social scientists were ready to study the slums and the economics of "actuary."

By the 1960s in American higher education a new "captains of industry" could have been written about. The businessmen and industrialists began looking to the college and university science departments and to the college administrators for direction, from the "researcher" in physics and chemistry to the social worker. What Franklin D. Roosevelt had begun intuitively and with compassion for college professors in dealing with the depression in the 1930s, President Kennedy carried to a science in presenting professors rather than businessmen for political leadership. Presently, there is little question about the relevance and vitality of the university to the organization of our civilized urban life. No city wants to be without an active "university complex" oriented to research any more than it would think of being without a police department.

The new power of the university is, interestingly enough, making its biggest gain in the core of the city. The city which in the mid-twentieth century was accused of losing its heart, its core, its logic for existence when the commercial-retail center of the city began to fragment to suburbia, ended once again in re-establishing itself, but this time around the learning center. The university provides a logical center because it has a multiple function now popularly referred to as the "multiversity." It is often, as already indicated, the largest single firm, in some instances with a direct and indirect employment center of a hundred thousand or more. It is the center of art and drama, of gigantic sports palaces. It is the producer of the most valuable product for the industrial city, i.e., skilled talent.

The headquarters for guiding the life of a great city like Boston, Minneapolis, or Philadelphia is increasingly centralizing in what is called the "university complex." Cities like Denver, Syracuse, Oklahoma City, Berkeley, and others have turned or are turning to the university to spearhead its search for new industries, new products, and cultural development in the community. In searching for the main artery of urbanism in the second half of the twentieth century, the leadership of the American cities will not find it any longer in the "downtown" retail center nor in the "business center." The past downtown of manufacturing or retail has been irrevocably dispersed to the fringes of the city. Even the political institution is organizing around the new nucleus—the university or rather "research and educational center." The power has in many instances already shifted, and the president of the university is now chosen with more care than any other person the community selects, whether for the major industry or the main political office.

Neither the universities themselves, nor the business and civic leaders of these cities are fully cognizant of what has happened in their cities. As Senator Fulbright has so aptly stated for foreign policy, the cities are operating on old myths and are not fully aware of the new realities. It comes as a shock both to the university and to the city that the university rather than the recipient of charitable donations by the previously realistic and practical "directors of destiny" of the city now becomes the caretaker of the city's future and destiny. The vital university now makes a vital city. Neither of these two is accustomed to this role and is somewhat frightened by it. "Rumblings" at the university, like that of Berkeley, once insignificant sidelights of a city's life, now cause critical vibrations throughout the entire state and nation. The university community is even more shocked and worried over its own impact, especially in the light of its traditional "ivory tower" relationship to the practical community. Questions of the wisdom of such a power and relationship are being raised extensively within the university community, but there is little possibility that it will reject the role.

The present disturbances from the gigantic and small "multiversities" throughout the nation are the birth pangs of a new force in the city and nation. There will undoubtedly be many more in all the universities in the country before the new relationship is recognized, rationalized and stabilized. A new relationship must be created to accommodate students who are themselves parents and even grandparents, for faculty who work for government or industry for a substantial percentage of their time, and especially to the university administrators who will be disbursing budgets bigger than any of the surrounding industry. Students who are in their twenties and thirties and who may have already been in higher education for five years or more cannot be treated in a sophomoric manner. They may be voters and expect the freedom of citizens to discuss the issues and participate in campaigns. They may be parents and taxpayers who are vitally concerned with the organization of government in their city or their nation. These are rights that are especially difficult to alter or suspend in any way for students who live off campus. However, even the campus resident student in an urban area cannot extricate his actions from affecting urban affairs when the university is so entwined with the welfare of the nation and the world. Faculty and college advisors will also demand a new responsibility and a higher return for their work. The power structure of nations will have to be modified to include this new element, and the university will have to undertake a responsibility that inevitably comes with power if it is to prevent chaos in the community.

The revolts from Berkeley to Columbia, from Michigan to Florida are therefore not to be mistaken, as they popularly appear to be, against the impersonal structure of the larger universities. Human relationships are just as intensive there today as they ever were at schools before. The student, even at classical Oxford, seldom saw or bothered to see a faculty member out of class; his tutor was his main contact. The crux of the rebellions is that universities have become central to the lives of the great majority of American people for both the physical organization of life and the spiritual and intellectual value of it. By 1985, we may expect as many forty-year-old students as twenty-year-olds. It is truly hard for us to believe that the factory, the traditional business firm, and the political organization are being superseded in importance by the "learning center."

The student in America is vital to the new urban society. The student at the university feels that he is preparing for something important, and most of all, he knows that he can be effective in revolt. This is not the sorry picture that alienation presents, where the lonely individual feels lost, apart, and insignificant in action. The present American university rebellions are more in the form of announcements that the students, graduate and undergraduate, part-time or full-time, young and old, are a significant new force in American society. The academic institutions from our top university administrators to the lowliest students are certain to be creative leaders of .tomorrow rather than the reflectors of yesterday. This is the new power of the university in America and throughout the urbanized world.

iii. *Schools of the Future*

One can now predict with certainty that the great majority of urbanized people will be connected with the universities most of their lives. If one were to plot this progression on some kind of Parkinson's Law we could predict that the majority of babies born in America today are destined to the educational institution from four years of age until sixty-five when they will finally be graduated and retired on Social Security. By then the Ph.D. will probably be replaced by several additional distinctions of academic recognition. The Nobel prize and other similar designations of achievement will cap the procedural orders or recognition.

This tendency to expand formal education is not unanimously accepted by any means. It may be seen by the skeptical as a monstrosity that needs to be curbed. Those who matured thirty years ago and who consider themselves hard-working and practical may view it simply as a dilution of education and a waste of taxpayers' money. All they can see is the growth of another bureaucracy feeding on itself, taking twenty years to do something that could be done in half the time. To ask for more school time is a waste. Too much of the students' time, they claim, is taken up already by frills like sports, speech, and the socialization of the child, all of which, the argument goes, could be done more effectively outside the school. Now there are not many who would want to decrease the present school time, but if one scans the literature on schools, one finds a good deal of antipathy to them, which has unfortunately caused a mood of suspicion among the general public followed by a reluctance to support them appropriately.

The generation maturing today sees the tendency to extend formal education indefinitely with optimism and sympathy rather with skepticism. The only real controversy they see is in regard to the kind of educational institutions which we are to construct to supplement those now in existence. Let us then ask ourselves two questions that are centrally relevant to the development of a continuing or advanced education, two terms which are being generally applied to the extension of school life. First, what are the conditions which provoke the extension of formal schooling? and second, what are the prototypes of the school beyond the present school structure?

The school today is society's formal organization which is increasingly our materially productive base and also attempts to keep pace with the preservation and use of knowledge. It tries to divide the task among administrators, research scholars, teachers and students so that by specialization they can bring the full impact of all knowledge on the problems at hand. The school may curtail time spent in the past on penmanship for more time to be spent on various types of mechanical symbols. It may also curtail the study of language vocabulary for an increased knowledge of mathematical symbols. Thus, the school attempts economically and sanely to deal with information beyond the capacity of the single individual.

Because of this new dual function it serves and because of the quantity of new information that must be ordered for use, we find ourselves confused about the purpose and function of the formal school system. Fortunately, because of the increased automated facilities, we are freed to spend from sixteen to twenty years devoting our time to accumulating, sifting and ordering information rather than to the production of those things needed for our physical necessities. Unfortunately for us, we have been unable to solve the relatively easier problem of devising the kind of school we need for the less interested or less capable of dealing with the present form of organization. We already have the physical capacity to withdraw fifty percent more of our population's time from production of our physical necessities, without decreasing that production. But our long established prejudices to maintain a social organization for production does not permit us an easy transition to an order led by education to administration, distribution and service.

We prefer to keep five million people out of industry and out of school, and we also prefer an even greater number loafing on the job, featherbedding, rather than to direct them to schools and pay for their education and make it personally relevant. By the latest reports of the Secretary of Labor regarding the situation of the unskilled, the student with only a high school education or less, is creating the biggest bloc of the unemployed in their age category. This is contrasted by the figures indicating great shortages of personnel in the higher educated and skilled categories. More disturbing is the failure to provide an additional education that is not and should not be on the basis of material productivity alone. We can now afford an educational organization that is relevant to leading and appreciating the "good life." This means organizing the acquisition of knowledge in the sense that it has always been one of the greatest human satisfactions, simply learning to "know" and to "understand." There is so much that all of us would willingly and enthusiastically pursue if it could answer questions for us as individuals. Among them is planned travel and exploration of the world around us. It is the exploration of the self in terms of talents possessed to be creative. This is the education that is satisfying and rewarding. It is one that we can increasingly afford. While its utility socially may be difficult to evaluate, it can be done as a contrast to the utility and indeed social cost of the unhappy and unemployed that roam our streets at present.

Let us now look at the second relevant question. What is the prototype of the new school? It would be insufficient simply to expand the traditional school system to take in those who are not effectively employed and put them in schools even though the solution would be saner than the one we now practice. The problem is re-education and continuing education, not only of the unemployed, but even more so for the financially successful, the busy professional, and the Ph.D. An even greater problem is the reorganizing of the educational system itself.

What are the prototypes of the new school organization? Only broad outlines can at present be identified. Since the university in the widest context is to become the new sovereign of urban organization, it will manifest itself in plural forms. This will not, however, detract from its central task, to educate the public to voluntarily support its order and its scale of values. The *Pax Universitas* will be with minimum violence and minimal political authority. The values will be universal humanistically, but regional physically. Membership in the university cities will depend upon acceptance as rigidly as membership in today's university.

It is difficult to appreciate that university-city units of have and have nots are to be any less subject to the habitational disturbances of today's national countries. The fact is that they will be more capable of peaceful organization, because they are highly interdependent and conscious of this bond. While this will not be a perfect guarantee against solutions by violence they will, nevertheless, come as close as human intelligence can direct.

More might be said about these cities oriented around educational systems. They will include every facet of the cities' organization. The organizational unit will change from a political City Hall type to university types. Linked together will be the libraries, laboratories, museums, hospitals and all industrial training programs. The function of the coordinated educational establishments will be to unify the larger society of citizens constituting the city's total inhabitants.

Notes: Chapter 10

1. Nevitt Sanford, ed., *The American College*, New York, John Wiley and Sons, Inc., 1962, p. 932.
2. William C. De Vane, *Higher Education in Twentieth Century America*, Cambridge, Mass., Harvard University Press, 1965, p. 2.
3. Clark Kerr, *Uses of the University*, Cambridge, Mass., Harvard University Press, 1963, p. 88.
4. David Riesman, *The Academic Revolution*, Garden City, New York, Doubleday Company, 1968, p. 13.
5. Kerr, *op. cit.*, p. 89.

11. THE SPHERE OF PRIVACY

The urban-universal world most characteristically is a world of great numbers of people, living in close quarters, highly susceptible to social contact and social surveillance. Since man is probably more inclined to sociability than withdrawal, this is a condition that he will uniformly welcome more than deprecate. Yet man is not a goldfish and he needs withdrawal from the social realm, he needs privacy. Since privacy like clear water and air was a substance that until recently was in abundance, and was taken for granted, we have little appreciation of the concern that will be given to this area in the urban-universal world. There are signs that we are becoming conscious of invasions of privacy, the need for it, etc., but these are still in very exploratory stages.

i. *Increased Surveillance*

George Orwell's novel, *1984,* was among the first to make us fearful of the day when mechanical invention and urban living would be able to put every American under twenty-four-hour surveillance. In his world we would not be able to hide. The nightmare of Orwell is an unlikely thing. However, at the same time, there can be little doubt that our personal and public life in urban collectivities is rapidly coming under increasing scrutiny. Those that hold any public trust are perhaps most keenly aware of it, but it is, at the same time, enveloping every

176

common citizen who votes, every person who works, everyone who joins an organization, everyone who is born.

Writing, printing, photographing, the preserving of records has made the urban-universal world possible. There can hardly be reason for doubt that it will not continue to determine our civilization. A sophisticated urbanism brings multiple new ways of preserving records and making them easily accessible to most people. When a baby is born in a hospital, which is becoming a universal occurrence of urban life, an intricate chart is prepared regarding the baby's features and parentage. A birth certificate is filed with the government. When the child is old enough, he goes to school where his activities are charted weekly or monthly regarding, ability, deficiencies, sociability, etc. At the same time, the family doctor keeps a record of the child's health. The family itself keeps a record (photograph album) of the gradual growth of the child. Someone in the neighborhood may have a movie record of some of the child's activities. The voice will be preserved on records and tape. Newspapers of some type or other are certain to find something about most people that they will print sometime.

As the child reaches adulthood, the process of recording its life becomes intensified. Employment means a detailed survey of nearly everything to the Federal, State, and local governments. They open credit accounts which dig further into their private life. They may join the VFW, Y.M.C.A., Rotary, Kiwanis, Civil Liberties Union, Elks, JCs, Socialist or Communist party, etc. All organizations are anxious to record their activities. Their lives are continually recorded in voting and press statements. They are kept under the watchful eye of the telephone and picture window.

Yet the above methods of recording are primitive compared to the recent developments in television, wire and wireless recording devices. Reading about them staggers the imagination regarding the endless ways they can be used. Television, the newest of the devices, is still in the explorative stage regarding its versatility. So far the TV camera's eyes have been focused primarily on trained actors and actresses, or on a public anxious to have their faces and actions visible a thousand miles away. The roaming TV camera is still set up only for spectacles like a queen's coronation, a president's inauguration, a hurricane, or a war.

What unlimited possibilities are becoming available in the closed circuit TV can be determined only by a guess at those few already in use. A local factory with closed circuit TV permits a watchman to watch a nineteen inch screen inside a gatehouse which he doesn't have to leave. A microphone and radio speaker installed at the gate permits the watchman to talk, listen, and see the employee who wants to enter without being seen himself. By electrically controlled switches the watchman opens the gate or refuses entrance. Similar systems have been installed inside factories to observe the employees in action. Printed reports indicate that they are even in the employees rest rooms so that check can be kept on those who spend too much time there. Department stores, supermarkets, anyone menaced by an excessive amount of stealing, can easily be induced to consider their use.

While wire and wireless sound and recording devices have been with us now for several decades, the new uses they are being employed to were only a fantasy in a Dick Tracy cartoon a few years ago. Now such things as a small wrist or pocket radio receiving set are becoming standard equipment in several professions. Doctors, salesmen, businessmen in Long Beach, California, may subscribe to a radio service wherein they are kept under continuous contact by carrying a seven inch receiver in their pockets. This permits the service to keep in constant touch regardless of whether the doctor is on the golf course, in his auto, or taking a walk. A more common device already well known to public school teachers and office secretaries is the intercom. This permits the school superintendent or office boss to check constantly on his personnel.

Government investigations in wiretapping have revealed uses of the wire and wireless recording devices so fantastic that the common citizen had not even read about them in the comic strips. During the investigations, testimony was given regarding the possibility of phone tapping without the necessity of cutting into the line. There was also discussion of parabolic microphones that could be aimed with a telescopic gun-sight to pick up a conversation three hundred yards away. The government investigation of wire tapping concluded that it would be increasingly harder in the years ahead to achieve individual privacy if you knew something that somebody else wanted to know, whether in national defense, business matters or private affairs.

Another area of recording that is generally obscure to the public but has recently grown into big business is that of the private investigator, more colorfully known as the "private eye" industry. According to recently published data, there are now at least 5,000 agencies in the United States, employing 150,000 people and taking in $250 million a year. Most of this industry has grown in the past fifty years.

Finally, there is a type of recording that on first thought

appears unimportant and insignificant to the individual, the anonymous poll. Even though some of us register our name with these recorders, we do it with the understanding that it will never be used against us. While these polls vary in approach and reliability, as a total they have produced a vast store of representative records. The polling in depth by all the social scientists have delved deep into our attitudes, desires, and actions. Thousands of noted psychiatrists, psychologists, political scientists, and economists have recorded American buying habits, sex habits, religious habits, etc., down to the type of tooth paste we use, cigarettes we smoke, books we read, etc.

Another facet of the mass urbanized living is that personal actions once up to the idiosyncracy of the individual now are matters of public concern. Urban living means a very strict regulation on sanitary behavior; you are regimented regarding animals in your home or yard, the removal of garbage and waste, the contamination of air, the making of noise. Despite these restrictions the nuisance is still greater in the extent to which any of these can still disturb the privacy of the family next door.

ii. *Americans More Self-Conscious*

Historically speaking, most of this loss of privacy has occurred only within the past fifty years. There are those among us whose early years were unaffected by this multi-surveillance. We in America are more likely to be conscious of these new mechanical recording devices for at least two basic reasons. First, the mechanical techniques are most highly and extensively developed here in America. Second, until the past few years the whole nation was party to an anonymity that was possible by the existence of an enticing frontier which quickly obscured the past and gave one a chance to start a new life. This was a situation unknown for many centuries in the settled Old World.

Frederick Jackson Turner recorded the end of this frontier back as far as 1890, but in reality it persisted down into the thirties. For while the physical reality of the frontier may have ended around that date, the idea of it existed in the minds of people until they saw those whom they had known had gone, come back, even to a loss of face, possibility of a prison sentence, or of the depression. Only then did they begin to conclude and consider the idea that they had to face and live with their surrounding conditions and their past, which their neighbors and increasing official recording were beginning to know. There now was a turning inward, a gradual acceptance of the fact that people would have to begin and end at the place where they were. They would have to follow a philosophy suggesting a search for opportunities in their own back yard—even amid depression and despair. Instead of running away from the undesirable conditions they would have to begin living with them. This at the same time would enhance the collecting and preservation of traditional records, plus the multiplication of new techniques. Now an uncooperative neighbor who kept his yard with filth would be regulated by the passing of an ordinance. If he failed to control his children, another ordinance would take care of them. If he was out of work, there would be a greater cooperation between himself and his co-workers. Unions could solve the problem which the individual prior to that would have done himself by demand, or by pulling up stakes and leaving. The government and unions would record their activities.

By the end of World War II with the tons of governmental war recording this increased surveillance through old and new techniques was being recognized. The postwar years of subversive investigations made us conscious of its pervasiveness. As in Abner Dean's cartoons, man was standing naked in his own back yard, with neighbors from all directions peering at him. His bathroom, bedroom, kitchen, and office were open to all. There was a decreasing possibility to hide. What a tremendous strain on us who had in the past known anonymity, privacy, and embarrassment by this type of exposure.

iii. *The Functions of Privacy*

What is being lost when the traditional private behavior is reduced? Insofar as records are the new invaders of privacy, there apparently has been a great deal of traditional privacy in society until the last sixty years. This, in part, is explained by the absence of facilities or need for extensive recording until we have a highly mobile society with very fluid property. It is also evident in the origin of the word privacy. It came from *privat* meaning to be deprived of something. This something was a public significance. Therefore, it appears to be a condition which was not recognized as desirable before. There was more than enough of it. In the terms of economists, people were ready to exchange privacy for something more scarce; that is, publicity and public significance. As pointed out earlier, relatively few people have been deprived of record privacy in the history of mankind. A better way of putting this is to say that the lives of few people were publicly significant enough to have their behavior recorded so that it could be widely known and judged. More information is now available on record regarding the small-town mayor than was on Shakespeare or George Washington during their lives.

The significance of privacy, or unguarded activity now that we realize a certain scarcity of it, is important to a social system and to the individual, for three reasons. One, it is essential to social and technical progress. Privacy provides for a kind of willingness or freedom to experiment and create. This is especially true if the experiment is contrary to accepted modes of behavior. Even if the experiment were not contrary to accepted modes of behavior, there would still be a likelihood, according to R. M. MacIver,[1] of a certain restraint on the part of the potential experimenter since the process itself may be subject to ridicule in its early and clumsy stages, especially if these were also potentially to be made public through records.

The extent to which a social system considers technical progress desirable and necessary, is the extent to which it will be necessary to provide a condition of non-recording. This does not mean absolute isolation and absence of any observation by other human beings. But it does mean an absence of a record which can potentially be used to manipulate the experimenter.

Second, each social system, of course, is interested in promoting its survival, but at the same time, ignorance of certain alternatives may be equally detrimental. Howard White points out in his analysis of privacy that it is essential in the operation of any political system which expects to promote the "study, discovery, and teaching of the political good. . . ."[2] It is thus necessary to question the present practices and to inquire into possible alternatives which may be contrary to the status quo. These alternatives might be very essential to survival under certain conditions, of at least, in the traditional sense of John Stuart Mill's liberalism, these alternatives are essential as a challenge to the status quo to prevent it from becoming too rigid and complacent.

Third, privacy provides a challenge for each individual by exposing to him his insignificance, the meaninglessness and futility of his actions. On the surface, this might not appear to be such a benefit. But the defenders of this condition, Lasswell and Arendt, contend that such a personal encounter with futility is the very anvil on which a meaningful personality can be hammered out.[3] I have no reason to question this and history is resplendent with heroic figures from Moses to Thoreau who vindicate such a condition of privacy. The retreat into anonymity has often been the basis for a true rebirth.

iv. *Urban Surveillance and Some Possible Benefits*

There is no doubt that man needs a certain degree of privacy to be creative, to feel care, to identify the true self, but the central question is whether he needs as much as he has possessed traditionally. The answer is undoubtedly that he does not, and a decrease of traditional privacy may have some salutory effects upon the urbanized man. During the period of the revolution from the agricultural to the urbanized society, man probably increased his privacy, his anonymity to a degree never experienced in history. He was easily able to escape from the farm-neighborhood community into the early urbanizations which were hardly conscious of his existence. He became a unit of production; and when he ceased being that, he very often ceased having any place in the city. His privacy of the self was even better disguised. No one knew the complete individual. The city provided multiple ways in which the individual could associate, but these were all in segmental units. The city worker divided himself between family, recreation, occupation, social club, etc., all of these concerning themselves with only part of the man, none of them taking in the whole person, seeing all these roles tied into some kind of a total self. Thus privacy or rather the possibility of this type of anonymity may have contributed to one of the great richnesses of the revolutionary period, the conflict of the self, the split personality, the illness of anomic so capably described by Erich Fromm.

The benefits that may be derived from this increased surveillance therefore can be extensive if it forces us to try to work out a personality wherein the different selves we have at least recognize their existence, and then work toward an effort of integration. Who can tell but that Freud and psychoanalysis as practiced today would be outmoded among such integrated personalities, or at least it might be carried on once again by those who study the society's codes of morality rather than forms of insanity. It would be small surprise if traditional religious organizations would become a greater force in personality formation than they have recently.

Although we are considering a new benefit resulting from surveillance, man's experience has been varied enough to make a parallel for the sake of understanding. There should be no implication drawn that the nature of man is one that needs surveillance. However we can conclude that a certain degree of it may be functionally useful under conditions of urbanism. Historically, Western man's most obvious experience with the extent of surveillance that is developing today has been with reference to an all-seeing God, who punished evil and scorned duplicity. The comparison is here being made only on the psychological effects this idea has had on man's actions and attempts no argument with regards to God's reality. Western man at the height of the feudal period kept God's will as a basic ingredient for his actions. He might ask the question of whether a certain act was reasonable, whether it was acceptable to his family and friends, whether fortune or fame or power would accrue from the action, but he would apparently also ask himself whether God would approve of this. I can deceive all, including myself, but I can't deceive Him. He is looking over my shoulder whether I am at home, in a saloon or a cave. "Not a sparrow would fall to the ground without His knowledge of it." That man then did not base his decision on this as well as the other reasons may be disputed but I hardly think disproved. At the same time there is ample evidence that our daily decisions, even major ones in probably most our actions today, do not give much consideration to this surveillance of God. Whether this is the result of greater irreligiousness or simply confusion is unimportant to this thesis. I don't think our thoughts for action today generally go beyond "it is reasonable, will others approve, will fame, or fortune or power accrue, can I get away with it." This is one reason why the transition to a new mechanical "god of records" might not be an easy one.

Another historical area of intensive surveillance which has all but disappeared was the small community, the village, a society organized of primary group associations. Until the rapid growth of cities and the development of urban life in the latter part of the nineteenth century these communities dominated the life of Western man; more so in Europe, but to an important extent in America also. Paul F. Cressey in a perceptive study gives a good picture of such a community before and after. The heavy work in the community was done in cooperation. People worked together on an informal basis. Some residents knew everyone in the community, their business, marital status and the quality of their moral character.[4]

Here are then two historical instances of a close surveillance of Western man, perhaps closer than present records will become. Can either of these instances be considered as harmful or destructive to man's character? No argument is here being made regarding their influences on invention and production, but from the aspect of personal psychological integration and the effects on individualism, both of which are assumed by the author as desirable characteristics. Personal integrity was almost a natural result from this close supervision, but the present fear of regimentation was almost absent. Instead the character from the primary community who was also God oriented was considered a self-reliant individual, independent and possessed of intense feeling of individualism.

The second general area that this increased surveillance, the god of records, may affect our character is through the invasion of privacy as illustrated by the few examples given previously. Perhaps most significant for the consideration of this aspect is the biological question, whether humans are a type of animal that must hide, retreat and have privacy. In the consideration of this point, it is useful to look at the kinds of acts that we wish private: Our bodies, our bodily acts, sex relations, excretions, outbursts of joy, sorrow, and apparent insanity. Yet are not these the very acts we do every day in the presence of other persons, especially in the life of a family? Have these acts tended to make us fearful of our wives, husbands, brothers or sisters? Haven't we instead felt more secure with them? Furthermore, there appears to be no loss of dignity when humans are caught in a situation like the military service where strangers are a part of our privacy, and then what privacy did the individual early man have?

The biological aspect, however, is not the one that most of our critics challenge when they talk about the need for privacy. Furthermore, they could justly point out that while bodily privacy is not an absolute necessity to the dignity of man, they could defend it along lines as a very satisfying and beneficial luxury when practiced. A luxury which will permit an intimacy with only a few people. An intimacy which will permit one person to enter the soul of another, labeled by many as one of the most pleasant relationships, and out of which grows love. They can point out that this luxury of privacy is also needed for the individual to retreat from other humans so that he can contemplate and examine his own soul—the kind of retreat which Lewis Mumford in his book *The Culture of the Cities* states is becoming possible only in the toilet today.[5]

There is no denial of the value of intimacy with a few people and of the cloister type of retreat for the individual. There is meant, however, a criticism of the great amount of prudishness which has developed to its highest point in the civilization of Western Europe known as the Victorian period, the condition of which is still partly with us. The period of the closed doors, a solid door in every room in the house, and even two in some; the period of heavy and all-covering clothes which once led the scantily clad Indian rebel Mahatma Gandhi on a visit to the self-adorned English King to remark about his nakedness in the presence of the King, that the King wore enough clothes for both of them. This was also the period which developed a privacy etiquette that prevented a husband and wife from seeing each other's body throughout the whole of their married life. A period which brought up a generation that could hardly imagine that some people could ever smell, or have sex relations, even though they may have laid claim to half a dozen offspring. This was a situation of privacy that many accepted as civilization and progress, as the only logical and natural development.

The amazing thing is the rapidity with which such etiquette became fast engrained in a culture. Lewis Mumford traced the beginning of this privacy to the late seventeenth century, and then, the development was primarily among the upper classes where the desire for it also developed slowly. The nineteenth century suddenly made it a fetish among all. From a situation in the seventeenth century where in Italy maidservants slept on trundle beds at the foot of their masters' and mistresses', in France where the bed was in the living room, to a situation where in most of Western Europe, and especially England and America a lady would not show her ankle.[6]

From the extremes of the animal openness to the Victorian secrecy there is a certain amount of privacy that is needed to produce characters that are self-reliant, individualistic and integrated. This unquestionably should belong to any individual upon request, unless he has committed a crime, and even then to be treated with dignity. There should be no necessity of locked doors within the house, bulky clothes, or a house in the middle of the desert. One should be able to obtain his privacy by simply informing his friends of his desire, and have the courage to expect it. This is a kind of privacy etiquette that can be developed even under great surveillance. Even though your problems may be known, you still demand the pleasure and sorrow that is needed in working them out, and the personal satisfaction of accomplishment that may accompany such action. At the same time greater ingenuity is likely to result from such freedom.

While to this point there is a defense of this new surveillance and suggestions of its possibility to promote integration and individualism, the author does not wish to minimize all the dangers which are so well demonstrated in today's literature and serious writing. There is as there always has been a threat to democracy. The police state, the *1984* of Orwell, is possible and a democratic nation will have to face this threat as it did the elite state of fascism or of annihilation through war. There is a danger from concentrating power and responsibility for the sake of efficiency. There is also an evident tardiness of responsible behavior with the use of records, especially in not being conscious of the time element and milieu of certain acts, which when portrayed without the time element creates an unfortunate and unfair picture. Perhaps there needs to be a growth of the concept that an individual is never alone on trial, but also the accuser, the prosecutor, judge, jury, and witness. This book, however, is not meant to develop any specific technique for individual action in a society permeated by a god of records. There are, however, a number of developed systems of behavior for growth in this type of society without the loss of individuality and integration of character. A brief statement of their points of applicability is sufficient here.

v. *Four Royal Roads*

In all four cases the authors are dealing with the individual of today who is threatened to extinction by "groupism" and regimentation, who has become lonely, full of dread and anguish because he has lost purpose, and even the method which permits him to become an individual in the mid-twentieth century. These authors are also fearful of the old type of callous individuality and pragmatic philosophy which had developed along with it because this type of individualism is at least out of place with the times. Majorie Grene in her book *Dreadful Freedom* states that pragmatism really celebrated a false individualism, the "adjusted individual, the stereotyped individual, the individual who has forgotten how to be an individual."[7]

The four authors who have developed royal roads to individuality in an urbanized system are Ortega y Gasset, Erich Fromm, Jean Paul Sartre, and David Riesman. While these men do not exhaust the field of those who recently have developed a method of education for the preservation and development of individuals, they have given the subject ample consideration and have presented an understandable method.

According to Ortega y Gasset in his book *Revolt of the Masses,* the society which is to be rich for human experience and development must be guided by an active minority who are composed of individuals, and who understand, recognize and support each other. This minority is not the elite of communist Russia or a fascist Germany, but a gathering together of people who are first individuals who seek each other's company for support and challenge. Their common coincidence with the other individuals is that they have separated themselves from the masses—dared to take the hard road and be different. The only effect records need to have on these courageous individuals is to make them better known.[8]

The path to individualism that Erich Fromm develops in *Escape from Freedom* comes from a group that will educate their children to develop a spontaneity of behavior. Each individual has a unique self which can act in ways other than those molds we try to impose upon our children. Repression of thought and spontaneous activity in areas like sex and death by our society in the past has caused a weakness in the ability to create, be truly individualistic in other areas. Development of the unique individual through spontaneity of action can become the aim of society under surveillance as much as under any earlier period.[9]

Jean Paul Sartre, the French existentialist, has probably best exposed the path to individual freedom in the *Paths to Freedom* trilogy and some of his plays, the exposition of which can be found in *The Flies*. Man is faced, according to Sartre, with an undetermined, godless world; the system of civilization is human, and our acts and beliefs are human. The realization of this frees a person to become the author of his self. There need hardly be any further realization since there is no pretense but that the records are in human hands and humans will determine their use.

The most recent and appropriate since he deals with the American scene specifically is David Riesman. His books, *The Lonely Crowd* and *Individualism Reconsidered,* give one an understanding of the nature of our present social organization, and a specific path through which individualism may be realized. This is through the development of a competence in some area of play or recreation. By doing this the individual is likely to develop competence of judgment and action in other areas of life which in turn lead to autonomy and individuality. This seems not at all to be affected by records.[10]

All four of these are valid methods for development of individualism threatened by the present highly technological and collectivized world. They also appear valid in a society that is enveloped by a twenty-four hour surveillance of a "god of records" that is essential in this urban-universal world. There appears no escaping from this organizational structure but it is not as frightening in its controls as we might believe. A certain degree of anonymity and uncontrolled action is surrendered, but there is also a plus side of personal integrity and social stability.

Notes: Chapter 11

1. R. M. MacIver, editor, *Conflict of Loyalties,* New York, Harper Brothers, 1952, p. 139.
2. Howard B. White, "The Right to Privacy," *Social Research,* June 1951, p. 196.
3. MacIver, *Conflict of Loyalties,* New York, Harper Brothers, 1952, pp. 132–133; Arendt, *The Human Condition,* Garden City, New York, Doubleday Anchor, 1959, p. 64.
4. Paul F. Cressey, "Social Disorganization of Harlan County, Kentucky," *American Sociological Review,* June 1949.
5. Lewis Mumford, *The Culture of Cities,* New York, Harcourt, Brace, and World, Inc., 1938, p. 29.
6. Ibid., pp. 40–41.
7. Marjorie Grene, *Dreadful Freedom,* Chicago, University of Chicago Press, 1948, p. 28.
8. Ortega y Gasset, *Revolt of the Masses,* New York, W. W. Norton and Company, 1932. See Chapter VII on "Noble Life and Common Life, or Effort and Inertia."
9. Erich Fromm, *Escape from Freedom,* New York, Henry Holt Company, 1941, pp. 256–276.
10. David Riesman, *The Lonely Crowd,* New York, Doubleday Anchor Books, 1950, and *Individualism Reconsidered,* New York, The Macmillan Company, 1954. See Part 3 on Autonomy.

12. CONCLUSIONS—LIFE IN THE YEAR 2000

Mobility will be the tour de force of the urban-universal man. He will move as no human civilization has moved before. Man will move to such an extent that a third of the urban-universal community will be moving to new locations each year. It is now estimated that a fifth of the American population moves to a new location each year.

This mobility of person will, nevertheless, be a stabilizing condition for urban-universal man. The excitement of travel and seeing new places will itself decrease interest in building new cities and creating new things. It will also decrease appetite for acquisition, since things located in a given place generally contribute less to a mobile person than to a stationary one. The willingness to work longer for material things beyond those necessary for a modest livelihood will also be subject to serious competition from the pleasures afforded by travel, recreation, and the chance to enjoy these pleasures.

There will be a lust for travel, for seeing new historical places, for swimming in tropical climates and then for the winter sports in winter climates, all within short periods afforded by air communication. Life expectancy will not be appreciably longer than it is now. Thus, to satisfy this thirst for travel, recreation, and education, our American adult of the year 2000 will devote considerably less time to material productivity. Also a substantial amount of his energy will go toward the reconstruction of historical places, rebuilt because of a human interest in the genesis of man. Natural wonders will be preserved. Outer space will be a limited outlet for the more adventuresome but will not be a significant part of life.

One of the basic premises to be realized is that *motion* is not *revolution*. A plane moving toward an airport is not a revolution. The revolution in transportation came when man broke away from the use of the biological locomotion of human slaves, horses, and other animals to locomotion by various forms of mechanical energy, from the use of engines powered by oil, coal, or steam to the jets with more exotic fuels. The various fuels might within the transportation industry be continuously considered revolutionary developments, but the hundreds of different combinations of non-animal energy do not involve a great increment of change on the part of the individual. The same is true of the different forms of motor vehicles, from the various machines that moved on land and rails, to those on water, snow, or air. They were logical extensions for man to travel, and revolutionary forces for transportation. The airplane is no more revolutionary than a steamboat, or railroad engine, or the automobile. All reached higher and higher rates of speed, but for man and his movement on earth these have not been incredible after the introduction of motor power. Mechanized transport moved two or three times the speed of a fast horse, whether we talked about railroads, automobiles, or other land and water transportation. The air transit did fundamentally change distances and speed to make any place on earth easily accessible, but it does not promise to alter land urban organization already fixed by the land and water transport.

In harnessing this physical power a little over a hundred years ago man has also devised physical forms, physical slaves which we call machines to do his manual work for him. They produce economically and in great abundance the things which sustain life and make it more enjoyable. Increasingly man is able to perfect these machines so that his physical contribution can be almost entirely eliminated. The urban-universal man thus finds himself released from the work of production of things to a production of services for other humans. His work, insofar as it is work, a compulsory obligation of human effort, is to labor on himself and in providing services for other people. It is difficult to call some of this activity work. The twenty or so years one is asked to spend on his own education is a compulsion that historically would have been, for most, one of the great voluntary tasks the individual might undertake. Nor is public service any more of a burden.

The real revolution of urbanization occurred when the great majority began to have an option of not working full time for the production of their livelihood. The full flush of this revolution, which puts some of us into a state of panic and horror, is only becoming apparent in the present age of western development. A few of the avant garde, like the American hippies and various groups on welfare show us that a great number can quit work for production entirely. Yet even these unemployed continue to live in what is relative abundance. Thus, we must not confuse "variations on a theme" with revolution. Consequently, to suggest that stability is going to occur for the next several hundred years does not assume a limit of human action, innovation and variation. A human being, as an example, changes considerably in shape and form during the first twenty years of his life. In the following twenty years there are few changes, yet they are hardly unimportant. This second twenty years is when a person is usually most stable. It is also the period of maturity and growth that generally has provided the intellectual civilization of man.

It is this kind of physical and emotional stability which inaugurates the end of a revolution for urban-universal man. He is freed from considerable work for production, to enjoy the fruits of that production. He is free to ask the question of what as an individual he is to do with his life. Most of all, he finds himself free to enjoy life that is intellectually satisfying. This life of the mind and spirit will have as one of its chief characteristics the reduction of physical violence. War, which is a great provocateur of physical change, will be rejected as a means of altering social order and will be avoided like the proverbial plague. This limitation on the use of physical violence will certainly hamper man in varying his physical environment, but not limit the satisfaction of one of the most basic of human inclinations, the desire to see, hear and to know. He will not be limited in traveling all over the world and within the lifetime of the individual to experience for himself the beauty and wonder of our earth and somewhat beyond it. Thus, the maturity of urban-universal man will show great spiritual and intellectual creativity, a physical movement from place to place, never experienced by more than a wealthy and adventuresome few in the past, but it will severely hamper physical change of a revolutionary nature. This educational, spiritual, and recreational activity will satisfy a great deal of the curiosity for change that in the past manifested itself in physical violence and the changing of things.

There is no implication that the year 2000 would see any substantial decrease in the work commitment. The three-day weekend and a two- or three-month vacation, the year sabbatical, all most certainly will be available to a large number of people when the urban-universal stage is reached. But because of the need for making life meaningful some psychological needs for respect from other humans and perhaps most of all, to prevent an anarchistic chaos, we will demand some work from all. The work will to some extent be in production, even at the expense of efficiency. This would mean an emphasis on the value of craft and art done by hand. But to a greater extent the work will be in self-education, self-development, and in service to others. Half of the population will be students or teachers for some time while the other half will be caretakers of the body health, through recreation and medically oriented professions. The ideal of the "Golden Age" of the classical civilizations of the Greeks and Romans will be realized, but in a new setting.

BIBLIOGRAPHY

Andrews, Wayne, *Architecture, Ambition and Americans.* Glencoe, Ill.: The Free Press, 1964.

Arendt, Hannah, *The Human Condition.* Garden City, N.Y.: Doubleday Anchor, 1959.

Aron, Raymond, (ed.), *World Technology and Human Destiny.* Ann Arbor: University of Michigan Press, 1963.

Bell, David, *End of Ideology.* New York: Collier Books, 1961.

Bentham, Jeremy, *Principles of Morals and Legislation.* New York: Hafner Publishing Company, Inc., 1948.

Blake, Peter, *The Master Builders.* New York: Alfred A. Knopf, 1961.

Boulding, Kenneth, *The Organizational Revolution.* New York: Harper Brothers, 1953.

Boykin, Edward (ed.), *The Wisdom of Thomas Jefferson.* Garden City, N.Y.: Garden City Publishing Company, 1943.

Brinton, Crane, *A History of Civilization* (2nd edition). New York: Prentice-Hall, 1960.

Brogan, Dennis W., *The Price of Revolution.* New York: Harper Brothers, 1951.

Chase, Stuart, *Power of Words.* New York: Harcourt, Brace, 1953.

Childe, V. Gordon, *Man Makes Himself.* New York: Mentor Books, 1961.

Cox, Harvey, *The Secular City.* New York: Macmillan, 1965.

Dahl, Robert, *Who Governs?* New Haven, Conn.: Yale University Press, 1961.

Davenport, Russell W., et al., *The Permanent Revolution.* New York: Prentice-Hall, 1951.

de Tocqueville, Alexis, *Democracy in America.* New York: Vintage Books, 1956.

De Vane, William C., *Higher Education in Twentieth Century America*. Cambridge, Mass.: Harvard University Press, 1965.

Djilas, Milovan, *The New Class*. New York: Praeger, 1957.

Dore, R. P., *City Life in Japan*. Berkeley, Cal.: University of California Press, 1963.

Easton, David, *The Political System*. New York: Alfred A. Knopf, 1953.

Ferguson, Charles, *Fifty Million Brothers: A Panorama of American Lodges and Clubs*. New York: Farrar and Rinehart, Inc., 1937.

Fitch, James M., *Walter Gropius*. New York: George Braziller, Inc., 1960.

Fortune, editors, *U.S.A., The Permanent Revolution*. New York: Prentice-Hall, 1951.

Freud, Sigmund, *Civilization and Its Discontents*. London: Hogarth Press, 1930.

Fromm, Erich, *Escape from Freedom*. New York: Henry Holt Company, 1941.

Gardner, John W., *Excellence—Can We Be Excellent and Equal Too?* New York: Harper Colophon Books, 1961.

Gerth, H. H., and Mills, C. Wright, (eds.), *From Max Weber: Essays*. New York: Oxford University Press, 1946.

Giedion, Sigfried, *Space, Time and Architecture*. Cambridge, Mass.: Harvard University Press, 1946.

Gottmann, Jean, *Megalopolis*. New York: Twentieth Century Fund, 1961.

Grass, Norman, *A History of Agriculture*. New York: F. S. Crofts, 1925.

Grene, Marjorie G., *Dreadful Freedom*. Chicago: University of Chicago Press, 1948.

Gruen, Victory, *The Heart of Our Cities*. New York: Simon & Schuster, 1964.

Hagen, Everett, *On the Theory of Social Change*. Homewood, Ill.: The Dorsey Press, 1962.

Hoselitz, Bert F., *A Readers' Guide to the Social Sciences*. Glencoe, Ill.: The Free Press, 1959.

Hunter, Floyd, *Community Power Structure*. Chapel Hill, N.C.: University of North Carolina Press, 1953.

Kerr, Clark, *The Uses of the University*. Cambridge, Mass.: Harvard University Press, 1963.

Korzybski, Alfred, *Science and Sanity*. (4th ed.) . New York: Institute of General Semantics, 1958.

LaPolambara, Joseph, (ed.) , *Bureaucracy and Political Development*. Princton, N.J.: Princeton University Press, 1963.

Lerner, Daniel, *The Passing of Traditional Society*. Glencoe, Ill.: The Free Press, 1958.

Lerner, David, (ed.) , *The Human Meaning of the Social Sciences*. New York: Meridian Books, 1959.

MacIver, R. M. (ed.) , *The Conflict of Loyalties*. New York: Harper Brothers, 1952.

Mannheim, Karl, *Ideology and Utopia*. (Tr. Louis Wirth and Ed Shils.) New York: Harcourt, Brace, A Harvest Book, 1936.

Marshall, Alfred, *Principles of Economics*, (8th ed.) . London: Macmillan, 1938.

Merriam, Charles, *New Aspects of Politics*. Chicago: University of Chicago Press, 1925.

Mill, John Stuart, *Autobiography*. New York: Oxford University Press, 1958.

Mills, C. Wright, *The Power Elite*. New York: Oxford University Press, 1959.

Mumford, Lewis, *The City in History*. New York: Harcourt, Brace and World, Inc., 1961.

————, *The Culture of Cities*. New York: Harcourt, Brace, 1938.

Odegard, Peter, et al., *American Government*. New York: Holt, Rinehart and Winston, Inc., 1961.

Ortega y Gasset, Jose, *The Revolt of the Masses*. New York: W. W. Norton, 1932.

Orwell, George, *Nineteen Eighty-Four*. New York: Harcourt, Brace, 1950.

Osborn, Elloit, *Men at the Top*. New York: Harper Brothers, 1959.

Osborn, Frederick J. and Whittich, Arnold, *The New Towns*. New York: McGraw-Hill, 1963.

Price, Derek, *Science Since Babylon*. New Haven, Conn.: Yale University Press, 1961.

Ranke, Leopold von, *History of the Popes*. (Tr. Mrs. Foster.) New York: Harcourt, Brace, 1925.

Redfield, Robert, *The Primitive World and Its Transformations*. Ithaca, N.Y.: Cornell University Press, 1953.

Riesman, David, *The Academic Revolution*. Garden City, N.Y.: Doubleday, 1968.

——, *Individualism Reconsidered*. New York: The Macmillan Company, 1954.

——, *The Lonely Crowd*. New York: Doubleday Anchor Books, 1950.

Rostow, W. W., *The Stages of Economic Growth*. New York: Cambridge University Press, 1962.

Sanford, Nevitt, ed., *The American College*. New York: John Wiley and Sons, Inc., 1962.

Sartre, Jean Paul, *No Exit and Three Other Plays*. New York: Vintage Books, 1949.

Smith, Adam, *Wealth of Nations*. New York: Collier Press, 1902.

Tawney, Richard H., *Equality*. New York: Harcourt, Brace, 1931.

——, *Religion and the Rise of Capitalism*. New York: Harcourt, Brace, 1925.

Thomas, W. I., and Znaniecki, Florian, *The Polish Peasant in Europe and America*. Chicago: University of Chicago Press, 1918–1920.

Thompson, Victor, *Modern Organization*. New York: Alfred A. Knopf, 1963.

Veblen, Thorstein, *Theory of the Leisure Class*. New York: Mentor Books, 1953.

Watson, John B., *Behaviorism*. New York: W. W. Norton Company, 1925.

Weber, Max, *Protestant Ethic and the Spirit of Capitalism*. (Tr. Talcott Parsons.) New York: Charles Scribners Sons, 1948.

——, *The Theory of Social and Economic Organization*. (Tr. A. M. Henderson and Talcott Parsons.) Glencoe, Ill.: The Free Press, 1947.

Wernick, Robert, *They've Got Your Number*. New York: W. W. Norton Company, 1956.

Whitehead, Alfred N., *Science and the Modern World.* New York: A Mentor Book (4th printing), The Macmillan Company, 1953.

Whyte, William H., Jr., *The Organization Man.* New York: Simon & Schuster, 1956.

Young, Michael, *The Rise of the Meritocracy,* 1870–2033. Baltimore, Md.: Penguin Books, 1961.

Articles

Cressey, Paul F., "Social Disorganization and Reorganization in Harlan County, Kentucky." *The American Sociological Review,* June, 1949.

White, Howard, "The Right to Privacy," *Social Research,* June, 1951, p. 196.

Wirth, Louis, "Urbanism as a Way of Life," *The American Journal of Sociology,* June, 1938.

INDEX

204

DATE DUE

GAYLORD